Home Study Course
in
Quiltmaking

By

Jeannie M. Spears

American Quilter's Society
P. O. Box 3290 • Paducah, KY 42002-3290

Printed by IMAGE GRAPHICS, INC., Paducah, Kentucky

ACKNOWLEGMENTS

Thank you to my parents, *Francis* and *Elizabeth Gillett*, for lessons well taught.

Thank you to my husband, *Marvin*, for his support and help.

Thank you to our children, *Shannon, Darcey, Becci, Ben,* and *Maaren,* for teaching me even more than they learned from me.

Thank you to the *quilt teachers,* who share so generously, and the *quilt students*, who inspire with their enthusiasm.

Table of Contents

Introduction   6

Lesson One: Preparation   7
Fabric and Batting Required
    Yardage Required
    Fabric Selection
    Batting Selection
Recommended Supplies
Fabric Preparation
Cutting Guide
Lecture: Planning Color

Lesson Two: Quilting Patterns and Background Grids   19
Patterns:
    Star Flower
    Feathered Heart
    Wreath of Hearts
    Snowflake
Lecture: Enhancing Quilts with Stitching Patterns

Lesson Three: Hand Piecing   45
Patterns:
    Churn Dash
    Card Trick
    Bud Bouquet
    Ten-pointed Star
Lecture: Drafting Geometric Patterns

Lesson Four: Traditional Applique   69
Patterns:
    Sunbonnet Sally
    Overall Sam
    Traditional Tulips
    Grape Vine
Lecture: Designing Applique Patterns

Lesson Five: Machine Quilting   101
Patterns:
    Clamshell
    Daisy
    Star Trail
    Tulip Wreath
Lecture: Estimating Yardage for a Quilt

Lesson Six: Machine Piecing   **125**

Patterns:
> Desperation
> Log Cabin
> Cat's Cradle
> Seminole Star

Lecture: A Short History of Quiltmaking

Lesson Seven: Ethnic Applique   **147**

Patterns:
> Tulip Garden
> Maze of Hearts
> Chintz Applique
> Mola Butterfly

Lecture: Quilting Today

Lesson Eight: Trapunto and Shadow Applique   **171**

Patterns:
> Heart Ring
> Rose in Full Bloom
> Iris Garden
> Ring of Roses

Lecture: Where Do You Go From Here?

Lesson Nine: Contemporary Applique   **193**

Patterns:
> Rolling Hills
> Love Birds
> Blossom Beauty
> Celtic Rose

Lecture: Quilt Competitions

Lesson Ten: The Finishing Touches   **217**

> Section One: Making a Quilt with the Quilted Blocks
> Section Two: Constructing a Top and Then Basting It on a Frame

Lecture: Taking Care of Quilts

Introduction

Welcome to the Home Study Course in Quiltmaking! Making quilts has been important to women for various reasons during the last few centuries. Quilts were made out of functional necessity – as bed covers to keep families warm before manufactured blankets were available, and also out of emotional necessity – to express artistic talent in a way which did not threaten men, to add pattern and beauty to what were overwhelmingly drab and depressing surroundings, and to keep a tenuous hold on sanity when events became overwhelming. If the quilts were treasured by family members and handed down to future generations, they also became tangible evidence of the existence of grandmothers and great grandmothers who were not then forgotten.

Today, women (and men as well) are in the process of rediscovering what it was about quiltmaking that was so important to previous generations. Although quilts are no longer a functional necessity, making them still fills emotional and expressive needs in many ways. The purpose of the *Home Study Course in Quiltmaking* is to give you the skills and practice you need to become proficient in the techniques used in both traditional and contemporary work, so you can discover for yourself the satisfaction and opportunity for personal expression that quilting offers.

You don't need to be an expert seamstress to be a good quilter. In fact, you don't even need to know very much about sewing to use the Home Study Course. Each lesson introduces a different technique with a general discussion of the basics, and then step-by-step instructions are given for each of the four patterns included in the lesson. If you make one pattern from each lesson, you will be able to complete a wallhanging or crib quilt. If you complete all of the patterns in the Course, you will have a full-size quilt large enough to use on a bed.

The patterns in each lesson range from easy to difficult, with some challenges thrown in for good measure. If you complete them all, you can be confident that you have the knowledge and skill to make any design that you want to tackle. Each lesson also has a lecture section on related material for inspiration or future reference. Both hand and machine quiltmaking techniques are covered, some of which are designed for quick and easy results, and some for traditional heirlooms.

Instructions are given for both using the "Quilt-As-You-Go" method, which does not require a frame, and completing the lessons as a quilt top, which is then stretched, basted, and quilted on a frame. If you are just beginning quiltmaking and aren't sure you will enjoy it enough to invest in a frame, the Quilt-As-You-Go method will let you quilt the entire piece in small sections in your lap.

One advantage of the Home Study Course is that you can work at your own pace, whenever you have time, learning as much or as little as you like, as fast as you like. Another advantage is that all of the material presented is written out for you so you don't have to depend on your memory to recall exactly what the teacher said to do or how to finish your project.

Remember that working through the Home Study Course is a learning experience. You will have to decide for yourself how much of a perfectionist to be. I seldom recommend that students do a completed block over, even if they are dissatisfied. If you already knew how to do everything well, what would be the point in taking the course? Including not-quite-perfect blocks in a quilt will also let you see your progress and compare final blocks against the first ones. However, if you are very frustrated or disappointed in the results, by all means try again. The block is sure to be better the second time!

Home Study Course
in
Quiltmaking

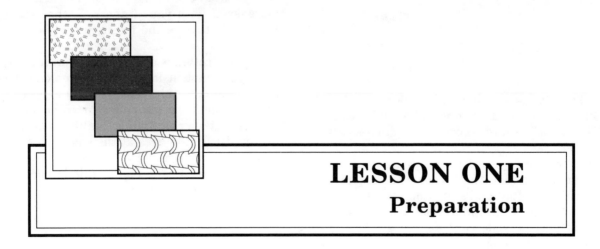

LESSON ONE
Preparation

LESSON ONE: PREPARATION

FABRIC AND BATTING REQUIRED

Before purchasing fabric, read the following section on desirable characteristics and color. If you plan to construct the top in one piece and then baste it on a frame and quilt it, the fabric requirements are given in Lesson Ten: Section Two.

Yardage Required

For a *wallhanging* of one block from each technique:
- 4¼ yards for background, border and backing.
- ½ yard each of a coordinated solid and small print, or 4 "fat quarters" of coordinating fabrics.
- 1 yard of a coordinated print for setting squares. (You may want to delay purchasing this fabric until the blocks are completed and you have a better idea of what color you want.)
- ⅓ yard cotton voile (optional, for shadow quilting: see Lesson Eight).
- Crib size batting, 40" x 60" or larger.

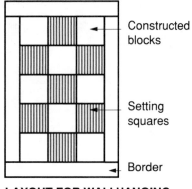

LAYOUT FOR WALLHANGING

For a *full-size* quilt of all 32 blocks:
- 12¼ yards for background, border, and backing
- Five or six ½-yard pieces of coordinated solids and prints.
- 3¾ yards of a coordinated print for setting squares. (You may want to delay purchasing this fabric until the blocks are completed and you have a better idea of what color you want.)
- ⅓ yard cotton voile (optional, for shadow-quilting: see Lesson Eight).
- ¼ yard of chintz with floral motifs. (optional, see

Lesson Seven, Pattern C: Chintz Applique).
- Batting, at least 80" x 100".

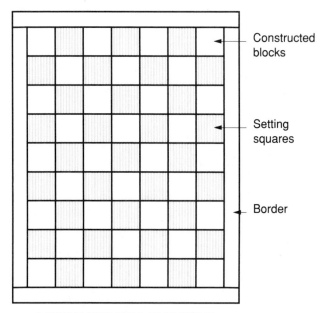

LAYOUT FOR FULL-SIZE QUILT

Fabric Selection

The best fabric to use for quiltmaking is a lightweight fabric with a smooth finish, such as broadcloth, with as much cotton in it as possible. If the fabric contains too much polyester, the applique will be difficult. Test the fabric by trying to crease it with your fingers. If the crease is sharp and stays in the fabric, it will be easy to work with.

If 100% cotton is available in your area in the colors you want, it is preferable to blended fabrics. If local fabric stores don't carry a good selection, try a mail-order supplier. Many advertise in *American Quilter* and other quilting magazines. See the list of resources at the end of this lesson for more information.

The lecture at the end of this lesson covers how to choose the colors for your quilt.

Batting Selection

A perfect quilt batting has not yet been invented. I would suggest using a stable, but not bonded, polyester batting. (If this is not available in your area, try mail-order sources.) Be very cautious of battings sold off the roll. Most of them are very crisp and springy, making it difficult to quilt easily. Unbonded battings with loose fibers are also hard for beginners to use, since they require great care in unrolling to get the thickness even.

If you use dark-colored fabric and a polyester batt in your quilt, you will probably find that some of the batting fibers migrate through the fabric giving it a "linty" appearance. This is often called "bearding" and it happens to a greater or lesser degree with all polyester battings I know about. It is just something quilters put up with to have the ease of care and quilting that polyester provides.

Cotton and wool battings are available in some areas, but need to be quilted more closely than polyester batts. If you are just starting out, you will probably be happier using polyester.

RECOMMENDED SUPPLIES
- Needles: Betweens, size 9 or smaller
  Sharps, size 10 or smaller
- Pins
- Matching thread
- Thimble or other finger protection
- Fabric scissors and paper scissors
- Rotary cutter and mat
- Rulers
- Fabric marking pencils
- Template material
- Masking tape
- Paper
- Seam ripper
- Emery bag
- Marking board
- Light box (optional, for use with dark fabrics)

Needles: Use the best needles you can get. It's worth it for ease of stitching. If small ones are not available locally, see the mail-order suppliers.

Betweens are used for stitching the three layers of a quilt together. You may also find them called "quilting" needles. Size numbers get larger as the needles get smaller. Start with a size 9, and as you develop a rhythm of stitching use smaller needles and your stitches will automatically get smaller. English and Japanese needles are finer than "dime-store" brands, and come as small as 12's.

Sharps are used for piecing and applique. Try to use size 10 or 11. They are somewhat difficult to thread, but are so fine they seem to slip through fabric. See Illustration 1-1.

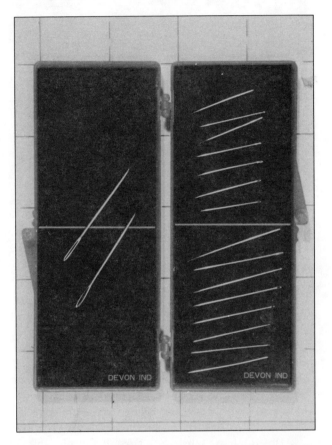

Illustration 1-1: Tapestry needles (left) for cording (optional) in Lesson Eight, Betweens for quilting (top right) and sharps for piecing and applique (bottom right).

If your needle seems to get sticky during stitching, dust your hands with cornstarch or talcum powder, especially in summer. An *emery bag* (often in the shape of a strawberry attached to a tomato pincushion) will sharpen your needles if you run them through it occasionally.

Pins: I prefer *glass-headed* pins, small ones for piecing, applique and machine stitching, and long ones for pinning three layers. They are quite visible, even in batting, and reduce the chance of unpleasant surprises from forgotten or unseen

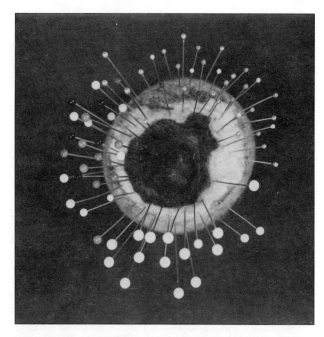

Illustration 1-2: Glassheaded pins, large and small.

pins when you are finished. See Illustration 1-2.

Thread: *Use any thread that is the right weight and color for your purposes.* I don't recommend using "Quilting" thread for a variety of reasons. It isn't any stronger than ordinary sewing thread, some of the colors fade, and worst of all, some of the colors run. Its major advantage is the glaze which makes it easier to thread, but it is too heavy to go through the eye of a needle smaller than a 10.

Do not use "Quilting" thread for piecing or applique, because it is too heavy. Use a good quality sewing thread, either cotton or cotton-wrapped polyester.

Thimbles: Quilters often have sore fingers on the hand which goes under the work to return the needle, because it's too clumsy for most people to wear a thimble to protect the underneath fingers, but it's silly not to wear protection on the stitching fingers. Although I have occasionally met people who quilt without any kind of thimble, you will be much better off, and be able to stitch for longer periods of time, if you make the effort to learn to use one.

You *can* get used to a thimble if you wear it all day for several days. If a metal or plastic one is too uncomfortable, try a leather one. A leather

thimble is flexible so you can feel the needle, and it will adjust to the shape of the finger.

Another option is the quilting "paddle" which you hold to push the needle with. See Illustration 1-3. My fingers can't tolerate a metal thimble, so I have learned to use a paddle. It did take practice, but it also improved my stitch. If your local quilt shop doesn't carry paddles, try the mail-order resources. If you just can't find anything you can use, try dipping your fingers in a solution of alum or rubbing them with the juice of the Aloe plant after a day's quilting. This is also good treatment for the fingers you use underneath.

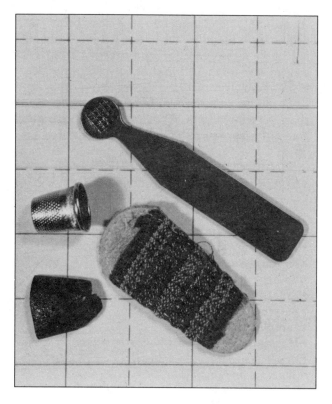

Illustration 1-3: Metal thimbles, leather thimbles, and the quilting "paddle."

Scissors: Purchase the very best scissors you can afford. They are a lifetime investment and make a big difference in your piecing accuracy and your pleasure in quilting. You will want an 8" pair for cutting fabric and a small embroidery pair for hand sewing. I hang the small pair around my neck on a piece of elastic so it won't get lost. Be sure to use the good ones *only* to cut fabric. Have an old pair handy to use on paper, plastic, and batting. See Illustration 1-4.

Illustration 1-4: Fabric and embroidery scissors and a pair of clippers.

Rotary Cutter and Mat: This recently introduced tool is invaluable to quilters. It enables you to cut simple pieces far more accurately, and faster as well. The mat is necessary to avoid ruining the edges of the cutter and to protect the table

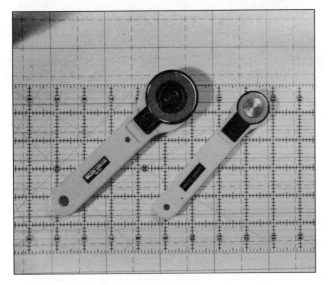

Illustration 1-5: Rotary cutters in two sizes, gridded ruler and cutting mat.

surface. You will also need a cutting ruler (see "Rulers"). *CAUTION:* The rotary cutter is a dangerous tool! *ALWAYS* replace the cutting guard before setting it down, and *NEVER* let children handle it. See Illustration 1-5.

Rulers: A clear plastic ruler with a grid printed on it is very useful, as is a cork-backed metal ruler. If you have a rotary cutter and mat, you will need a wide *gridded ruler*, preferably 6" x 22", to use with them. It is even more useful if it has angle lines.

Several devices are also available to mark ¼" seam allowances on fabric, including plastic rods and circular "rollers."

Fabric Markers: You will need an assortment of pencils to mark fabric; light-colored leads for dark and print fabrics, and darker leads for light fabrics. I use a micro-lead mechanical pencil (0.5mm) with 3H or 4H lead for most marking. Such pencils are available at stationery or drug stores. I

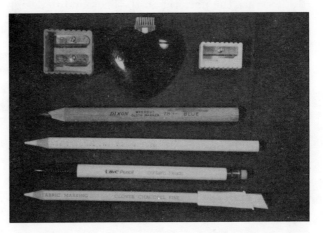

Illustration 1-6: Marking tools for light and dark fabrics and pencil sharpeners.

also like washout pencils or white pencils to mark dark fabrics. They are available at quilt shops. See Illustration 1-6.

Template Material: Templates are used to mark patterns on fabric. Any sturdy, easy to mark and cut material can be used for templates. Some materials are, in order of preference:

Template Plastic: Most quilt shops carry transparent or translucent plastic sheets that can be marked with a pencil and cut with a scissors. The advantages of plastic are that patterns can be traced, and that the edges and corners won't wear down with repeated use. It's definitely worth the investment.

Fine Sandpaper: Since it doesn't have much body the corners will wear down quickly, but templates made out of it won't slip on the fabric if you put the rough side down. It is suitable for patterns which don't have a lot of identical pieces.

Light Cardboard: If cut from cereal boxes or manila folders, it is very inexpensive but it poses the same problem as sandpaper. If you need to mark many pieces, you must cut several accurate copies of the same template. You could glue sandpaper to cardboard to make it a little sturdier; then the template won't slip on fabric.

Other Materials: Old X-ray film, Shrink Art™ sheets, heavy acetate, sheet tin or aluminum may also be used for long-lasting templates, but they are difficult to mark and cut accurately.

Paper: You will need sheets of paper at least 10" x 10" to trace the patterns in the book and to design your own. Shelf paper or freezer paper is inexpensive and easy to find. Large tablets of vellum or tracing paper are even better to work with and the paper lasts longer. Easiest to use is a pad of accurate 12" grid paper, available from quilt shops.

You will need *freezer paper* for several of the techniques in the Home Study Course.

Masking Tape: A roll of ¾" wide masking tape will come in handy for fastening patterns and fabric so they don't slip, and for marking straight lines for quilting. It is also available in a ¼" width for marking quilting lines on pieced blocks.

Seam Ripper: It's a good idea to have a small seam ripper on hand in case you make a mistake that you can't live with. Look for one with a fine point.

Emery Bag: This is often in the shape of a strawberry attached to a tomato pincushion, but you may also be able to find one sold separately. It is used to keep needles sharp and smooth.

Marking Board: To make marking fabric easier, glue a piece of fine sandpaper, rough side up, to a rigid backing such as cardboard, plywood, or foam-board. Place the fabric you are marking over it and the fabric won't slip.

Light Box: (optional) You will need a light source underneath patterns if you want to trace them on a dark fabric. You can tape the pattern and fabric to a window, although that tires my arms quickly. Some other options are:
• separate the leaves of a table and put a piece of glass or acrylic over the opening and a lamp underneath.
• use the front of a TV, which is turned on but is between channels.
• if you have a light in your washing machine, put a piece of glass or plastic over the top and use that.
• put a piece of acrylic plastic over the top of a cardboard box and plug a socket into an extension cord for an inexpensive light source.

RESOURCES

The following magazines have information on mail-order suppliers:
American Quilter, published by the American Quilter's Society, Box 3290, Paducah, KY 42002-3290.
Lady's Circle Patchwork Quilts, published by Lopez Publications, Box 7655, Teaneck, NJ 07666.
Quilter's Newsletter Magazine, published by Leman Publications, Box 394, Wheatridge, CO 80034-0394.
QUILT, published by Harris Publications, 1115 Broadway, New York, NY 10010.

GENERAL INSTRUCTIONS

FABRIC PREPARATION
If you plan to wash the quilt, wash the fabric before using it!

If you have chosen any dark or strong colors, test them for colorfastness before washing them with other fabrics or using them in your quilt. There are a number of ways to test.

- Baste a small piece of white fabric to a small piece of the colored fabric, and then get them wet. Let them dry, remove the white piece and compare it to the piece you cut it from.
- Wet a white piece of fabric and rub it on the surface of the colored fabric.
- Place the colored fabric in a white bowl or sink and add water.

If any of these methods show that the color runs, wash the piece separately until no more color comes off. You can also try adding salt or vinegar to the wash water to set the color.

If none of the fabrics run, you can wash them all together. When you dry them, *don't use a fabric softener sheet* in the dryer. It can leave greasy spots on the fabric. It is easiest to take your fabrics out of the dryer before they are bone-dry, shake them to get out major wrinkles, and then iron them dry.

CUTTING GUIDE

After you have washed and ironed the fabric, first cut the background blocks, borders, and backing. It is a good idea to do it all at once, before you begin working on individual blocks, to be sure you have enough fabric and have cut it correctly. If you find it necessary to get more, you are more likely to be able to.

Although it is tempting to rip the fabric for the large pieces, I don't recommend it for two reasons. One, the threads may pull, ruining the edges, and two, few fabrics will rip at right angles to the selvage, so the blocks will not be square. Use a ruler to mark the pieces, then cut them or, better yet, use a rotary cutter and mat to get absolutely accurate pieces. Remove the selvages before cutting the fabric.

Border, Background, & Backing Fabric

Use the diagrams provided to cut the borders, background and backing pieces if you are using the Quilt-As-You-Go method to construct your project. Use leftover fabric in your blocks if you wish.

Note: If you want to construct a top to baste and quilt on a frame, read Lesson Ten for alternate instructions before you begin.

For the wallhanging, cut:
- (8) 16" squares
- (6) 11" squares
- (10) right triangles, height 12", base 24"
- (4) half-triangles
  (Mark (2) 12" by 36" strips. Mark the top of each strip 6" from its end, then every 24". Mark the bottom of each strip every 24". Connect the lines for the sides of the triangles.)
- Borders: (2) 6" x 60" and (2) 6" x 40"

16" squares 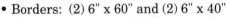 triangles: height 12"
base 24"

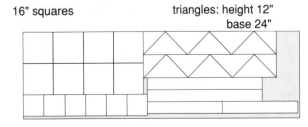

CUTTING DIAGRAM FOR WALLHANGING

For the full-size quilt, cut:
- (32) 16" squares
- (24) 11" squares
- (14) right triangles, height 12", base 24" (See instructions on page 13 for marking triangles.)
- (4) half triangles
- Borders: (2) 6" x 106" and (2) 6" x 85"

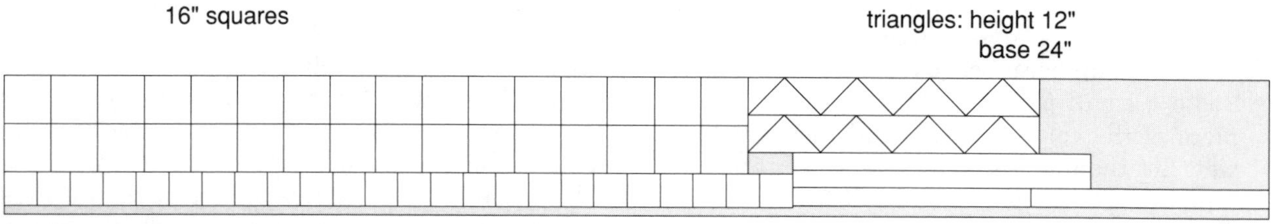

16" squares

triangles: height 12"
base 24"

CUTTING DIAGRAM FOR FULL-SIZE QUILT

Setting squares

You may wait to purchase this fabric and cut the squares until all the blocks have been constructed if you wish.
- Wallhanging, (7) 11½" squares
- Full-size quilt, (31) 11½" squares

Batting
- Wallhanging, (15) 14½" squares
- Full-size quilt, (63) 14 ½" squares

To cut the batting, use the rotary cutter; or make a 14½" square template (which you will also use later to mark the backing squares), mark the batting with colored chalk and cut it with paper scissors.

Using the Rotary Cutter and Mat
You can cut six to eight layers of fabric at a time with the rotary cutter. Fold the fabric in layers, place it on the mat, and use the cutting ruler as a straightedge to guide the cutter. If your mat has a grid, you can also use it to line up the ruler for larger measurements. If it doesn't, you will need to use pins to mark the placement of the edge of the ruler.

LECTURE: PLANNING COLOR

Many people lack confidence when it comes to planning the colors in a quilt. It's understandable, since a quilt is a major investment of time and money. You want to be sure you'll like it when it's finished. Talking about color on a black-and-white page isn't easy, but I'll try to give you some suggestions that might help.

First of all, and most important: trust yourself when you decide on colors. There is absolutely no *best* arrangement, and if two choices seem equally good to you, you'll probably like either of them as a finished quilt. For heaven's sake, don't use something you don't like very much. You may never finish the project if you do. There are so many choices available today, in quilt shops and through mail order, that you should be able to find a combination you enjoy.

Start with a Fabric

An easy way to plan the colors for your quilt is to start with a favorite fabric. The first step is to decide on a basic color—from the room the quilt is going in, the favorite color of the person you are making it for, or just a color you want to work with. The second step is to find a print fabric in that color. It helps if it has several additional colors in it. Use the print to find the rest of the fabrics for the quilt. Pull the bolt off the shelf and put it in your cart or set it on the counter.

Find a solid which is a deeper shade of the color the print looks when you view it from ten feet away. Add unbleached muslin, cream or a lighter shade for the background. Set the new bolts on top of the first one you chose. If you like the combination and are satisfied, you don't need to look any further. This is the safest method, but also the least interesting.

To make the selection more exciting, find a fabric in one of the accent colors of the print. This is often a contrasting color and will add more life to your quilt. You could choose another solid, or a second print with the first solid color in it for additional fabrics. Keep pulling the bolts and looking at them together before you make the final choice. See illustration above, right.

I would suggest that you wait to purchase the

Decide on a Color: BLUE

Find a print in that color:

Select a coordinating dark solid:

Select a light solid or unbleached muslin for background:

Select a coordinating print for the setting squares:

fabric for the setting squares until you have finished all the blocks and laid them out as a whole. If that process doesn't give you a clear idea of what color or kind of print you want to use, then take several of the blocks with you to the fabric store and lay them on various bolts until you find one you like.

Hints:

• An unbleached muslin or cream color is easier to use than white as a background color. White is a stark, harsh, and highly contrasting color and must be used carefully. Yellow is almost as difficult to use. If you like, you can use any soft solid color. Black and other dark colors are very striking, but difficult for beginners to work with, since they are hard to mark.

- Beware of using prints that have an unbleached or white background that is the same as the fabric you have chosen for your background. Not only will shapes in your quilt disappear because of the lack of contrast, but the print also tends to fade out at a distance. See Illustration 1-7.
- Be hesitant to choose all prints or all solids for a quilt. It is usually more interesting to vary

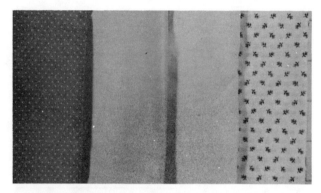

Illustration 1-7: Not enough value contrast.

Illustration 1-8: Better value contrast, but prints are too similar in size.

Illustration 1-9: Good range of values and print sizes.

prints and solids, sizes of prints, values of the colors (darkness), and intensity of the colors. Small prints give a soft, muted look at a distance, large prints look more vibrant, and solids intensify their colors. Look at fabrics from an arm's length, but also from across the room. Prints especially may change color at a distance. See Illustration 1-8 and 1-9.

- Be sure to look at the fabrics in natural light, away from fluorescents or shop fixtures. Artificial lighting can change colors dramatically.
- Colors can be sorted into two general groups, those with cool, or blue, undertones and those with warm, or yellow, undertones. In general, stick to one group or the other when you chose your colors.
- If you get stuck, quilt shops can be of great help in choosing fabric. Just don't let a salesperson talk you into something you don't really want.

Scrap Quilts

Scrap quilts can be an exciting challenge! If you're like me, you find it a sin to throw away any piece of fabric which might conceivably be used sometime. Family quilts made from leftovers of sewing projects can bring back memories to recipients. If you're not careful, though, you can end up with a jumble of fabrics and colors. Plan a scrap quilt carefully so that its colors relate to each other and values balance.

If you want to use scraps, first be sure all the fabrics are of the a suitable weight and fiber content. Test them by creasing them as described earlier. Large-scale prints and a wide range of colors are difficult to work with. You will probably be more satisfied with the results if you use smaller prints and stay in one color family, for example, all blues or all greens. Be sure to vary the value of the colors, using some light, some medium, and some dark. You should plan on purchasing the background, border and backing fabric.

One way to decide which colors go together is to build a color "tree." Dump all the fabrics you have to choose from on a table or the floor. Working on a neutral surface or a white sheet, pick out a print you really like and put it in an empty space. Pick out other prints with the same colors. Lay them one over the other like a hand of playing cards so you can see a little of each one. See the illustration on the next page.

Building a color tree

Then pick a color from the first print and find a solid to match it. Find all the prints that have that color in them. Fan them out over the first solid. Pick another solid from the second print, then find more fabrics to go with it. Continue to lay them out, lapping one over the other.

Keep going until you have enough fabrics or until you have used up all the ones that go together. Get on a chair or squint to see what they look like from a distance. (If you're near-sighted, take off your glasses). If you see any that look wrong or clash, pull them out. The remaining fabrics can be used in your quilt.

Be careful with large-scale prints. Strange things can happen when they are cut into small pieces, some interesting and some disturbing. Be sure to watch what is happening!

RESOURCES

For further color study:

Color and Cloth, Mary Coyne Penders, 1989, The Quilt Digest Press.

The Second Quiltmaker's Handbook, Michael James, 1981, Prentice-Hall, Inc.

The Patchwork Quilt Design and Coloring Book, Judith LaBelle Larsen and Carol Waugh Gull, 1977, Butterick Publishing.

Color for Quilters, Susan Richardson McKelvey, 1984, Yours Truly.

Home Study Course
in
Quiltmaking

LESSON TWO
Quilting Patterns And Background Grids

Pattern A: **Starflower**, *Beginner Level*

Pattern B: **Feathered Heart**, *Intermediate Level*

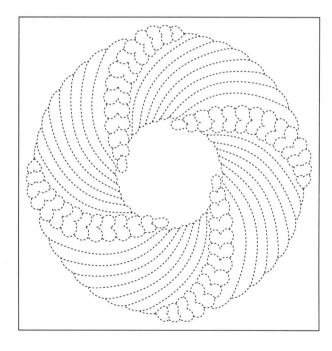

Pattern C: **Wreath of Hearts**, *Advanced Level*

Pattern D: **Snowflake**, *Challenge Level*

LESSON TWO: QUILTING PATTERNS
& BACKGROUND GRIDS

To use this lesson, first read its Introduction and its General Instructions. If you are making the wallhanging, decide which pattern you would like to make. Each one has the difficulty level indicated so that you can take into account your own skills, interest, and time. If you are making the full-size quilt, you will want to complete all of the blocks.

Note: If you want to construct a complete top and then use a frame to baste and quilt, see Lesson Ten: Section Two, then go on to Lesson Three.

INTRODUCTION TO THE
QUILTING STITCH

A quilt can be defined as a textile sandwich with layers of fabric on the top and bottom and a batting between them. The top may be pieced of smaller pieces of fabric or decorated with appliqued designs, or the design may result from the quilting pattern alone.

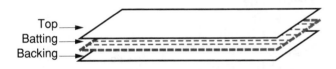

Running stitches which go through all three layers are used to hold them together. Before polyester battings were available, wool or cotton battings were used. It was necessary to quilt those materials very closely to prevent the filling

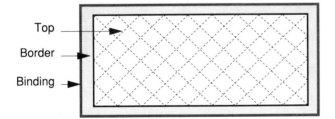

from shifting and pulling apart when the quilt was washed or cleaned. The tiny stitches added strength to the quilt, which was very heavy when wet. The amount of quilting that was required added a very desirable three-dimensional quality to the design of the quilt.

Although the polyester battings available today do not require such close quilting, the Home Study Course includes a lot of stitching patterns, for several reasons. One is that good quilting stitches come with practice. Another is that when you learn the relationship between the activity of your needle and the look and feel of the quilt, you will be able to recognize fine workmanship in pieces by other quilters. Also, it is the quilting that makes the finished product unique among the fiber arts, and you will want to emphasize that characteristic if you go on to develop a serious interest in quiltmaking. And last, but not least, quilting is my favorite part of quiltmaking.

Using a running stitch to quilt is very much like using a line to draw. The linear quality of the stitching is used to enhance and embellish the design of the top and add a third dimension. This linear quality of the quilting is subdued when an all-over design or grid is used. The texture of the grid emphasizes unquilted spaces and its regularity makes it perceived as background.

Three of the patterns in this lesson have a central design motif and a background grid to enhance it. The fourth pattern is very intricate, and needs an unquilted background as contrast. The motifs are of the type often used for alternate plain blocks in a quilt set like a checkerboard. Each of the grids contributes a different texture to the look of the block. You will find additional grids in the other quilting lessons. When you finish them all, you will have a "catalog" of effects to chose from in your own work.

GENERAL INSTRUCTIONS

Tracing the Patterns

The full-size patterns in this book are printed on facing pages with a slight overlap in the center. Using a dark fine-line pen, trace a complete pattern for each block as follows:

Prepare an accurate 10" square of paper from shelf paper, freezer paper, or tracing paper; or use a pad of quilt block graph paper, marking off the 10" square boundary of the pattern. If you are not using graph paper, fold the square in half to make a vertical crease.

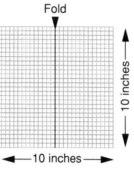

Place the left side of the pattern paper over the left side of the pattern in the book, using artist's tape or masking tape to secure it in place, matching edges and center crease with center line. Trace the pattern.

Carefully remove the tape and place the right side of the pattern paper over the right half of the pattern in the book, matching edges and the center line. Secure with the tape. Finish tracing the complete pattern.

Preparing the Backing Blocks

Use these instructions to prepare all the backing blocks. For the best results, work flat on a table when basting blocks.

If you didn't do so when you cut the batting squares, prepare a 14½" square template from plastic or cardboard for marking the seam line on the backing. Double check the measurements of all sides and the angles of the corners before using it. Mark the center of each side on the template.

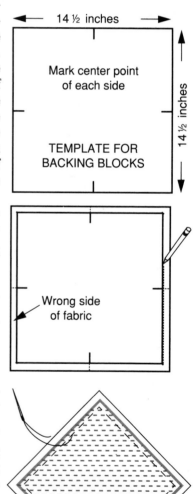

Center the template on the *wrong* side of a 16" square of backing fabric. Lightly mark around the template, making dots at the corners and marking the centers of each side in the seam allowance.

Place a 14½" square of batting on the backing square inside the marked lines. Baste the two layers together close to the edge of the batting.

Marking Quilting Patterns

Prepare a 10" square template for the patterned block, checking the measurements of the sides and angles for accuracy.

Center the template on the RIGHT side of an 11" square of background fabric. Lightly mark around the template, making dots at the corners.

Mark the quilting pattern on the RIGHT side of the background fabric, according to the instructions for each design.

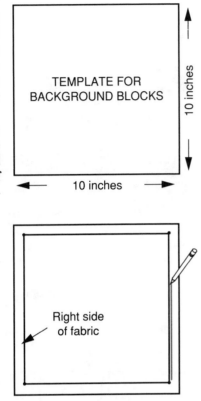

TEMPLATE FOR BACKGROUND BLOCKS

10 inches

10 inches

Right side of fabric

Basting for Quilting

Place the marked background block diagonally on the basted backing and batting, match-

ing and pinning the corners of the background block with the marks at the center of each side of the backing.

Carefully baste all layers together around the edges of the background block through the seam lines. Baste diagonally in both directions, then horizontally and vertically through the center.

Hint: If you don't knot the end of the thread, it will be easier to remove.

Quilting

The basic principle of quilting is to use a running stitch to hold three layers together – the top, batting, and back. It is very difficult to quilt without some kind of finger protection. A variety of thimbles were discussed in Lesson One, including metal and leather thimbles. If you are uncomfortable with the first one you try, keep trying new styles. You cannot put enough pressure on the needle to get through all the layers without a thimble of some kind.

Thread a *Between* needle, size 9 or smaller, with 18" of thread in a contrasting color. Use a single thread, keeping it short to avoid tangles and breaking. Although the majority of quilts are stitched with a thread that matches the background fabric, I strongly urge you to use a contrasting thread where indicated. Your stitching will improve quickly because your stitches will be easy to see. Don't expect that your practicing will look perfect at first, and don't worry about what the back looks like until you are satisfied with the front.

Fasten the end of the thread invisibly before beginning to stitch.

•Method 1: The easiest method is to make a small knot in the end of your thread. From the top side, insert the needle between the layers along the line you intend to stitch, ½" away from the beginning. Come out where you intend to start. Pull the thread until the knot rests on top of the fabric. Give a slight tug until the knot pops inside, and pull up gently until it is just under the top layer where you will begin stitching.

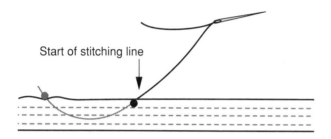

Start of stitching line

•Method 2: If you are an experienced hand stitcher, the following method is more difficult, but holds the end of the thread more firmly. Do not knot the thread, but begin by inserting the needle between the layers under the line to be stitched, coming up where you intend to start. Pull the thread through until it just disappears under the surface of the fabric. Begin stitching, taking two or three stitches. Pull firmly on the thread. If you have caught the end, it will not pull out. If it does, try again. It is most difficult to start this way on a curved line. If two tries don't catch the thread, use a knot as above.

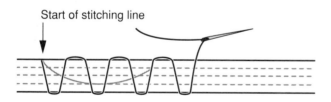

Start of stitching line

Use a running stitch and stitch on the marked lines. Try to make the stitches and the spaces between them on the top even. Many people find that the easiest rhythm develops when they take two to four stitches on the needle at a time. Look at the stitches on the needle before you pull it through the fabric, to be sure the spaces and stitches are even. Take the needle out and try

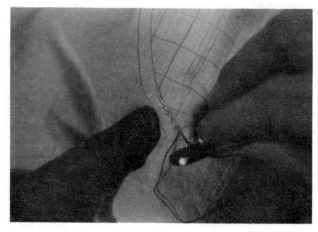

Illustration 2-1: Stitches on the needle.

again if you're not satisfied. See Illustration 2-1.

You must go through all the layers with every stitch. Hit a finger underneath with the needle each time you take a stitch.

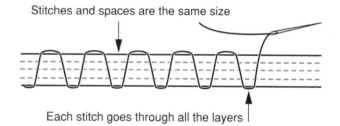

Stitches and spaces are the same size

Each stitch goes through all the layers

If you haven't done much hand sewing, aim for stitches about the size of Row A (Below). It is more important that your stitches be straight and even than that they be small. As you improve with practice you can aim for the size in Row B.

The hardest stitch to get even and straight is the one between pulling the thread out and putting the needle back in. If your stitching looks like Row C, try lining up the needle with the previous stitches as you insert it.

Row A

Row B

Row C

The size of your stitches will depend on the weight of the fabric and the batting.

To end a line of stitching, insert the needle

between the layers of fabric, back along the stitches you have made. Bring it up through the fourth or fifth stitch, and then insert it into that stitch again and run it through the layers in the reverse direction.

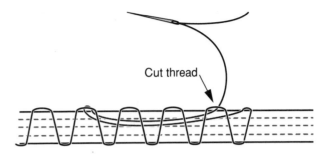

Cut thread

Hints:
- Stitching should generally start in the middle of the work and go out to the edges, whether you are working on a block or a quilt. If you have wrinkles, you will be able to release the basting and work the problem area out to the edge. Another option is to start at one edge and work to the other edge.
- Many people are most comfortable stitching in a counterclockwise direction with the work above their hands. If that feels awkward to you, or if you have trouble making your lines of stitching smooth, try working in a clockwise direction with the work below your hands.
- Try not to bunch fabric up in your hand when quilting. The batting is slippery, and the layers may slide. If you find it awkward trying to keep one hand underneath to receive the needle, pin the top edge of your block into a pillow or piece of foam rubber to stabilize it or use a block-size quilting frame or hoop. A 14" hoop will hold the blocks fairly well.
- Stitching should be flat. To achieve a three-dimensional effect, be sure to pull the thread taut enough with each set of stitches so the thread lies flat, not on the top and bottom. However, don't pull it so tight that you pucker or wrinkle the fabric.
- After you are satisfied with the way your stitches look on the top, turn the block over and look at the back. The stitches and the spaces between them should be even, although not necessarily the same size. If you have not taken a definite "bite" of fabric with each stitch, try

inserting the needle as vertically as possible each time you go through the layers, and be sure to hit the finger underneath. If the finger gets uncomfortably sore, try to hit the fingernail, use some kind of thimble, or rub your finger with the juice of the Aloe plant. Eventually you will develop a callus.
- Remove basting carefully when you finish. As you quilted, you may have caught the basting thread in the quilting. If so, *cautiously* clip it close to the fabric surface. (A slip of the scissors will cut your fabric, which will be difficult to mend. Clippers do not have as sharp a point as scissors.) After removing all the basting thread from the top, turn your work over and remove any remaining thread from the back.

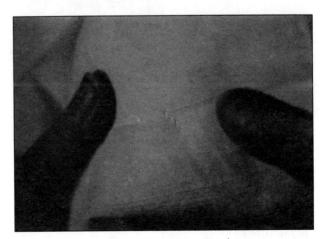

Illustration 2-2: The quilting stitch.

Pattern A: **Starflower**, *Beginner Level*

The background grid is often called the "Hanging Diamond." Because it is made up of evenly spaced straight lines, they can be stitched using masking tape or artist's tape as a guide, and no marking is required.

In addition to the line design of the quilting pattern, the area between the center eight-pointed star motif and the inner circle is filled with what is called "stipple quilting," a time-consuming but effective method of giving background texture. It is easy to distort the area, and the entire block as a result, by pulling the quilting stitches too tight, so be careful.

STEP 1:

Mark the pattern on the right side of a background block, following directions in the General Instructions.

STEP 2:

Baste the marked background block to batting and backing, following directions in the General Instructions. Add a line of basting near the double circle.

STEP 3:

Quilt the marked pattern with a contrasting colored thread. Begin with the eight-pointed star motif in the center. As necessary, slip the needle between the layers from the end of one stitching line to the beginning of another. Be careful not to let the needle come through the bottom layer, which results in "traveling stitches."

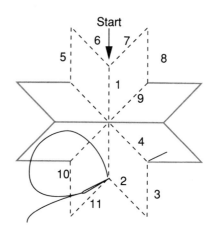

STEP 4:

Quilt the double circle.

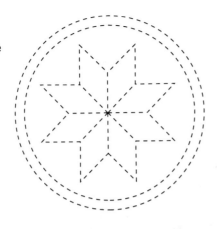

STEP 5:

Quilt the petals, stitching one layer of petals all the way around first, then stitching the other.

STEP 6: (*Optional*)

To stipple the area between the eight-pointed star and the double circle, use thread to match the background and stitch rows ⅛" to ¹⁄₁₆" apart, filling in the area.

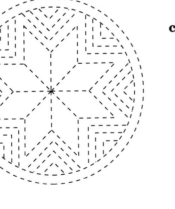

STEP 7:

To stitch the Hanging Diamond grid, use ¾" masking tape.

a: Lay a piece diagonally from corner to corner, centering it. Stitch on both sides.

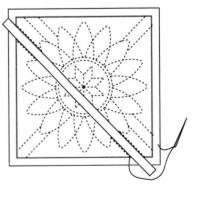

b: Lay the tape diagonally in the opposite direction, again centering it. Stitch on both sides.

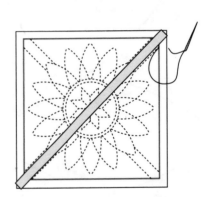

c: Pick up the tape and move it to one side of the stitched line and stitch the other edge. Continue to move and stitch along the edge until you have filled in the entire background.

Hints:
- Be careful not to extend stipple stitching over the inner circle.
- Use the masking tape as a guide, stitching a little away from its edge. Don't let your needle ride up and down the edge; the needle will get sticky and hard to use.
- Don't leave the masking tape on your block more than a short period of time. If left overnight or longer, especially in hot or humid weather, it will leave a sticky residue on the fabric.

Pattern B: **Feathered Heart**, *Intermediate Level*

Feathers are an elegant quilting design motif, often used to show off the skill of the quilt-maker. However, they need a background grid to show to best advantage. The close diagonal lines and inside diamonds of this grid make the feathers look individually stuffed.

STEP 1:

Mark a background block with the pattern, according to directions in the General Instructions.

STEP 2:

Baste the background block, batting and backing together according to the directions in the General Instructions. Add another line of basting near the "spine" of the feathers.

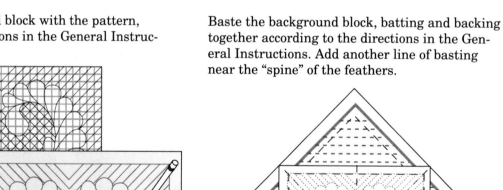

STEP 3:

Quilt the Feathered Heart with contrasting colored thread.

a: Begin with the teardrop shape at the top of the heart; then quilt the "spine" to the bottom and around one-half of the bottom heart.

b: Repeat for the other side.

c: Fill in the feathers along the spine, slipping the needle between layers to get from one to another.

STEP 4:

Quilt the background with matching colored thread.

FEATHERED HEART
PATTERN

FEATHERED HEART
PATTERN

Pattern C: **Wreath of Hearts**, *Advanced Level*

Since the quilting lines in this pattern are intricate and very close, a background grid doesn't enhance it visually.

STEP 1:

Mark a background block with the pattern according to the General Instructions.

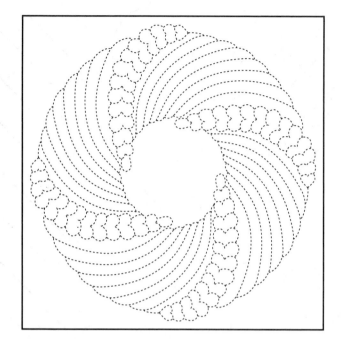

STEP 2:

Baste the background block, batting and backing according to the General Instructions. Add a line of basting near the inside and outside edges of the wreath.

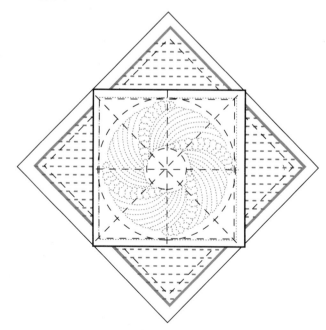

STEP 3:

Quilt the wreath using contrasting colored thread.

a: Begin by quilting the curved lines on either side of the heart sprays.

c: Quilt the remaining curved lines. Be careful when slipping the needle between the layers to get from one line to the next.

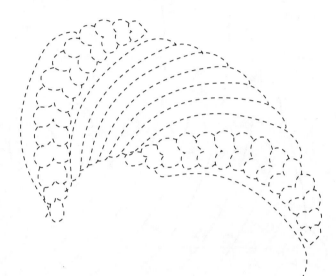

b: Then quilt the hearts.

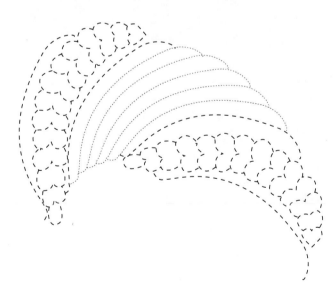

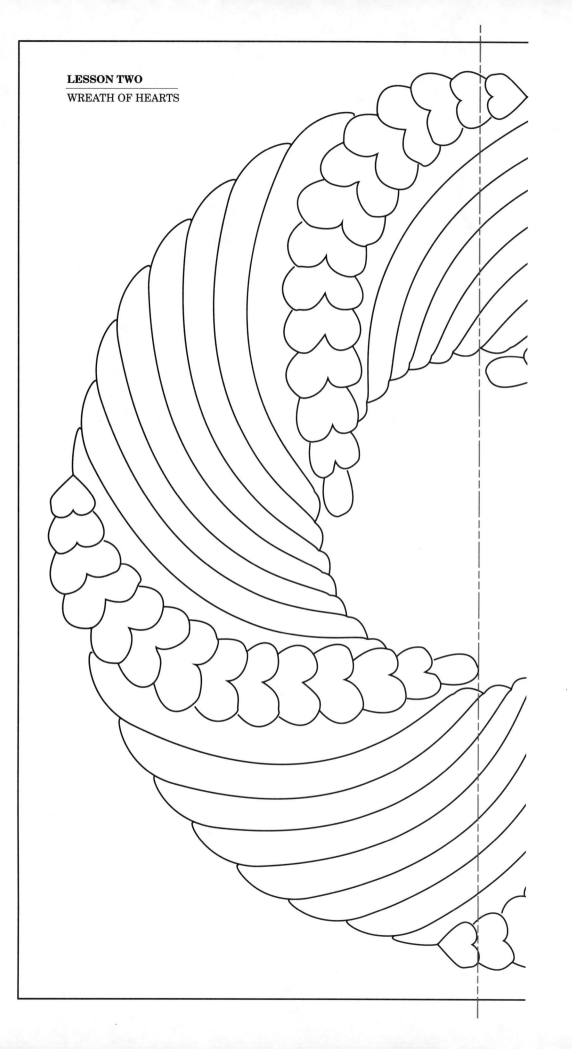

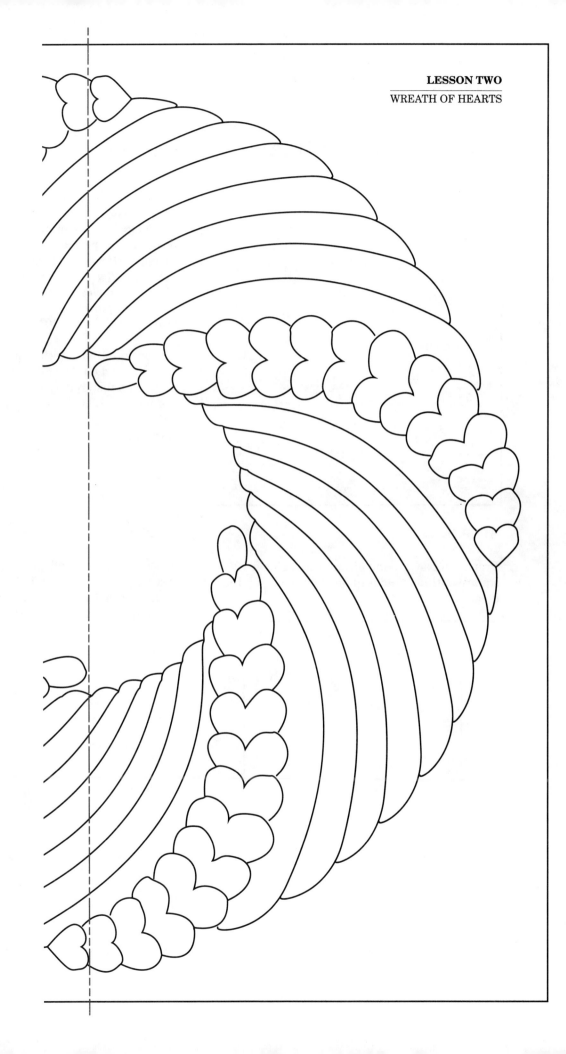

Pattern D: **Snowflake**, *Challenge Level*

The Snowflake design for this block is cut from freezer paper using paper folding techniques, a challenge because of its three-axis symmetry. The technique is used and taught by Anne Oliver of Virginia. (*If you don't want to do the paper folding, the pattern may be traced as for the other blocks in this lesson. When tracing, be sure to reverse the pattern across each fold, not rotate it, or it won't fit on the 10" square.*)

The background is "echo" quilted, a pattern traditionally used on Hawaiian quilts, and thought to have been inspired by waves along the shores of the Islands. Lines of echo quilting are usually ¼" to ½" apart, but the scale of this 10" block calls for closer lines.

STEP 1:

Prepare a background block by marking a 10" square outline. Fold it in quarters and iron the creases.

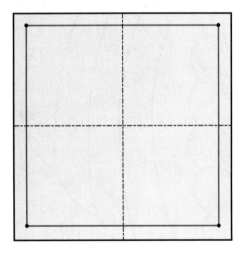

STEP 2:

Trace pattern 2D and cut out. Cut a 10" square from freezer paper. Fold it in half horizontally. Use pattern 2D to mark fold lines and fold in thirds. Fold again in half, so your paper matches the diagram.

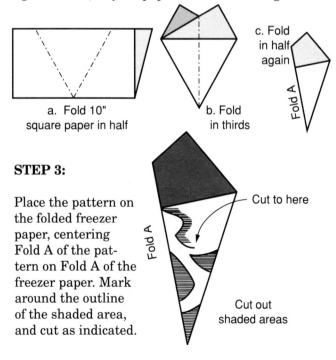

a. Fold 10"
square paper in half

b. Fold
in thirds

c. Fold
in half
again

Fold A

STEP 3:

Place the pattern on the folded freezer paper, centering Fold A of the pattern on Fold A of the freezer paper. Mark around the outline of the shaded area, and cut as indicated.

Fold A

Cut to here

Cut out
shaded areas

STEP 4:

Open to the half fold. Refold as shown, so that the 30-degree and 120-degree folds match and the ends of the horizontal fold match. Mark and cut the remaining portion of the pattern.

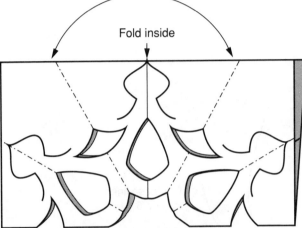

Bring together

Fold inside

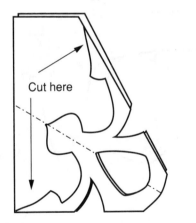

Cut here

STEP 5:

Carefully open the cut paper. Center it on the background block, shiny side down. Using a hot iron without steam, press it firmly to the surface of the block. The plastic coating will melt slightly, adhering it temporarily.

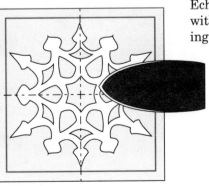

STEP 6:

Baste the background block with the ironed-on pattern to the batting and backing according to the directions in the General Instructions. Diagonal basting lines should go through the points of the pattern. Stitch right through the paper.

STEP 7:

Quilt around the edges of the freezer paper pattern using a contrasting colored thread. Remove the freezer paper. (If it tends to pull away before you are finished, which may happen on some fabrics, use pins or more basting to keep it in place, or mark around it with a pencil and remove it completely.)

STEP 8:

Echo quilt with matching thread.

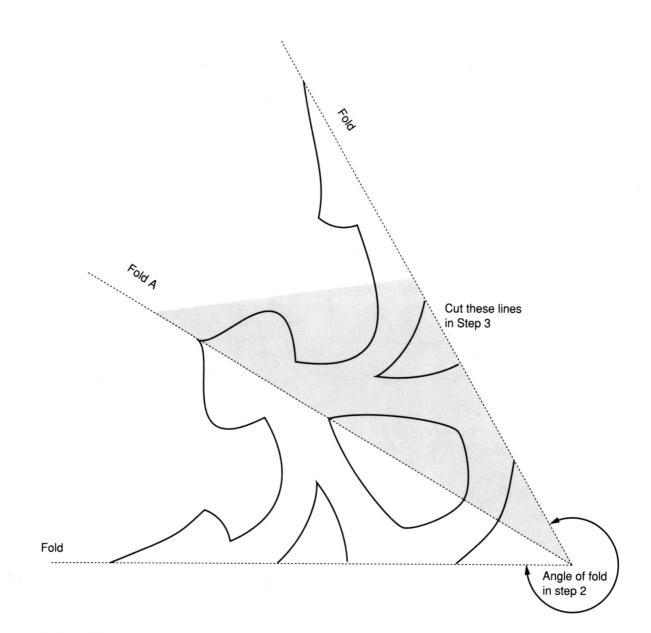

Fold

Fold A

Cut these lines
in Step 3

Fold

Angle of fold
in step 2

Pattern 2D

HOW ARE YOU DOING?

When you have finished your blocks, check them to see how well you are doing. Did your stitching improve as you practiced?

- Quilting stitches should be equal in length. If they aren't, check how they look on the needle before you pull it through.

- The spaces between the stitches should be equal to the stitches. Again, if they aren't, check how they look on the needle.

- Stitches should be in a straight line or smooth curve. If your lines wobble, try lining the needle up with the previous stitching as you take new stitches.

- The ends of the thread should not be visible. If you can tell where you started and stopped stitching, use more care. If knots have popped out, make them a little bigger.

- The thread should lie flat without puckering the fabric. If it is too loose, give a slight tug as you pull the thread through the stitches. If it is too tight, pull it through more gently.

- The stitches should come through evenly on the back. If you miss some stitches, try using a metal thimble or paddle to "rock" the needle as you stitch.

- The fabric and stitching should be even and smooth and not distorted. If it doesn't lie flat and smooth, you may be bunching your work up in your hands too much as you stitch. Try smoothing it out on a flat surface frequently as you work, or use a hoop or pin into a pillow.

- There should be no puckers, pleats, or wrinkles on the front or back where stitching crosses itself. This problem often results from inaccurate basting. Be sure your square templates are accurate and that you work flat on a table.

- Markings should not show. If you have used a lead pencil, try erasing the lines with a soft pink or white eraser. If you have used a washout pencil, dampen the lines and they will disappear. Use a lighter touch when you mark the next block.

- The block should be square, and no more than ½" of the original measurement should have been "taken up" with the quilting. If the block is not square, you will have trouble completing the quilt. You may even need to do it over. Don't worry if less than ½" of the original measurement has been taken up in the quilting. That will be accommodated as you put the quilt together.

LECTURE: ENHANCING QUILTS WITH STITCHING PATTERNS

Since three layers held together by stitches is the basic definition of a quilt, the design formed by those stitches is a major component of the visual image of the work. Planning the design should be given as much thought as the selection of piecing or applique patterns and choice of fabric and color. Just as the pattern of the quilt can be traditional, contemporary or innovative, the quilting design can show the same characteristics. Consider the effect you want to project with your finished quilt.

Traditional

Characteristics of traditional quilting patterns include outlining each piece of a patchwork block ¼" from the edge, stitching close to the outside edges of applique, and using a variety of background grids. Favorite motifs for fancy designs in plain areas are feathers, cables, and other intricate shapes. Traditional quilting designs leave no more than a square inch unquilted, because, as mentioned earlier, before polyester, batting would shift and lump if it was not firmly stitched down.

Contemporary

When polyester batting became available, it freed quilters from the necessity of stitching so closely, so contemporary designs tend to have a more open background grid if one is used, and patterns are more realistic. Pieced blocks are often stitched "in the ditch," right along the edge of the seam. Floral motifs and graceful open geometrics are used for plain blocks and borders, and designs can be related through common themes.

Innovative

Some quilters have pushed the freedom that polyester batting provides even further, developing quilting designs that contrast to or amplify the overall image of the quilt top. For instance, circular designs quilted over a square pattern like the Log Cabin give it an entirely different appearance. Quilting cloud or water patterns over a scenic design can give a very subtle texture to a piece, or realism can be enhanced by the quilt stitches.

RESOURCES

Traditional:

Quilting, by Averil Colby, 1971, Charles Scribner's Sons. A book packed with historical information and traditional designs.

Fine Feathers, by Marianne Fons, 1988, C&T Publishing. How to design your own feather patterns, mark quilt tops, and quilt.

Quilting Designs from Antique Quilts, by Pepper Cory, C&T Publishing. Interesting designs from old quilts.

Publications by *Marguerite Wiebusch*, Feathers and Other Fancies, Russiaville, IN 46979.

Contemporary:

Publications from *Dianna Vale*, 1294 32nd Ave. NW, Salem, OR 97304. Dianna has published several books of very graceful realistic, floral, and geometric designs.

Also:

How to Improve Your Quilting Stitch, by Ami Simms, Mallery Press. Step-by-step instruction, well illustrated, of the author's prize-winning technique.

Home Study Course
in
Quiltmaking

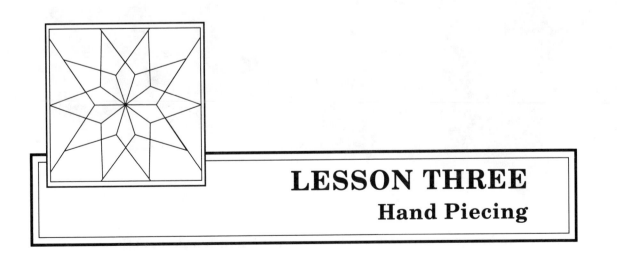

LESSON THREE
Hand Piecing

Pattern A: **Churn Dash**, *Beginner Level*

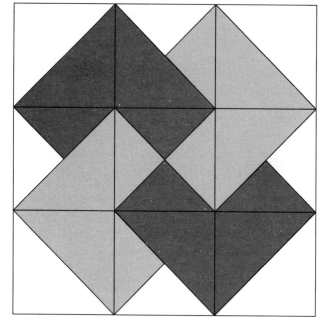

Pattern B: **Card Trick**, *Intermediate Level*

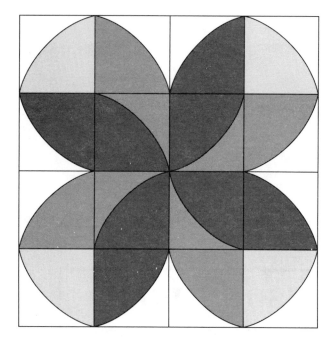

Pattern C: **Bud Bouquet**, *Advanced Level*

Pattern D: **Ten-Pointed Star**, *Challenge Level*

LESSON THREE: HAND PIECING

To use this lesson, first read its Introduction and its General Instructions. If you are making the wallhanging, decide which pattern you would like to make. Each one has the difficulty level indicated so that you can take into account your own skills, interest, and time. If you are making the full-size quilt, you will want to complete all of the blocks.

Note: If you want to construct a complete top and then use a frame to baste and quilt, see Lesson Ten.

INTRODUCTION TO HAND PIECING

As mentioned earlier, there are three basic categories of quilt construction; pieced, appliqued, and all-quilted, sometimes called "white-work" or "whole cloth" quilts.

Probably the majority of the quilts made in the past, and even today, are pieced quilts. Perhaps they are popular because they can use up scrap pieces of fabric too small for other projects, or because the shapes used are simple and geometric and lend themselves to graphic visual impact, or because the repetitiveness of the block shapes makes constructing them relaxing. There is real satisfaction in slowly but surely stitching together small pieces of fabric to create a thing of beauty.

One-Patch Blocks

Squares   Rail Fence   Triangles

Hexagons   Spools   Clamshells

Traditional pieced blocks are divided into categories based on how they are constructed. One-patch blocks use just one shape; a square, triangle, rectangle, or hexagon, any shape that will fit together to create a flat surface. There are even patterns based on circular shapes, such as Spools and Clamshells.

Two-patch blocks are squares or triangles with a "bite" of various shapes taken out of them. The most common is the "Drunkard's Path" and its relatives.

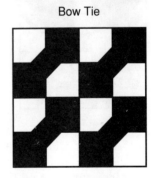

Hearts and Gizzards   Drunkard's Path

Orange Peel   Bow Tie

Four-patch blocks are squares subdivided into four smaller squares, and nine-patch blocks are squares subdivided into nine smaller squares.

Double Four-patch   Ohio Star

The smaller squares are again subdivided into squares, rectangles or triangles.

Nine-patch

Single Irish Chain

Shoo-fly

Five-patch and seven-patch blocks are named for the number of divisions along one side of a block (possibly because it's clumsy to call them "25-patch" and "49-patch").

Wedding Ring

Sister's Choice

Bear's Paw

Dove In The Window

Another classic shape for pieced quilts is the 45-degree diamond, which is used to make eight-pointed stars and all their variations, up to quilt-size stars such as the Lone Star and Star of Bethlehem.

Eight-pointed Star

LeMoyne Star

Blazing Star

Rolling Star

Narrow strips of leftover fabric which were too small to use for anything else were stitched together to make "string" quilts, the most common of which is the Log Cabin in all its infinite variations.

Log Cabin

Courthouse Steps

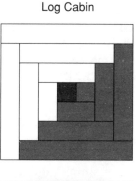

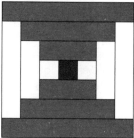

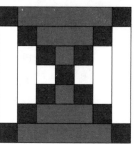

Cornerstones

Pineapple

The next time you look at a pieced quilt, see if you can discover the basic block, and whether it falls into one of these categories.

RESOURCES

Patchwork Patterns, Jinny Beyer, 1979, EPM Publications, Inc., McLean, VA.

The Quilt Design Workbook, Beth and Jeffrey Gutcheon, 1976, Rawson Associates Publishers, Inc., New York, NY.

The Pieced Quilt, Jonathan Holstein, 1973, Galahad Books, New York, NY.

The Standard Book of Quiltmaking and Collecting, Margaret Ickis, 1949, Dover Publications, Inc., New York, NY.

The Quiltmaker's Handbook, Michael James, 1978, Prentice-Hall, Inc., Englewood Cliffs, NJ.

The Sampler Quilt, Diana Leone, 1980, Leone Publications, Santa Clara, CA.

The Curved Two-Patch System, Joyce M. Schlotzhauer, 1982, EPM Publications, McLean, VA.

For block identification:
The Quilt I.D. Book, Judy Rehmel, 1986, Prentice Hall, New York, NY.

GENERAL INSTRUCTIONS

This lesson covers basic hand-piecing techniques. They are not difficult to master, but you must be accurate at all stages to succeed. Even a variation of less than ⅛" on each shape you stitch will mean a difference of 1" or more in the finished block.

The most important thing to remember is to work carefully and accurately. Try to find a quiet spot where you can spread everything out, especially when you are making the templates and marking the fabric.

Placement of Fabrics

Before you start cutting or stitching, you need to plan the arrangement of your fabric in the block. Trace the block diagram included in the instructions for each pattern and use colored pencils or felt-tip pens to try different arrangements of your fabrics. Color it as many ways as you can think of. When you have found an arrangement you like, proceed to construct your block.

Illustrations using three fabrics are given at the beginning of each pattern to give you an idea to start with, but you may use more fabrics, place the lights and darks in different positions, or arrange your fabrics any way you wish.

Making Templates

Templates for *hand-piecing* are made the size of the finished shape and do not include the seam allowance. Most pattern diagrams you will find in books and magazines are also "finished size." This is because the most important line to mark on the fabric for hand-piecing is the *stitching* line. The ¼" seam allowance will be added when the pieces are cut from the fabric.

Trace the pattern pieces for the block you are going to construct on lightweight paper and cut them out, using a ruler to keep lines

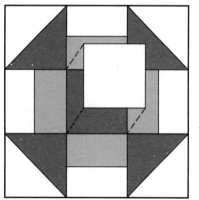

straight and a sharp pencil. *(If you are using translucent template plastic, lay it over the patterns and trace them directly; then skip to STEP 3.)*

When you cut out the pieces, cut just *inside* your marked line, so when you mark around the shape with a pencil, the pencil line is the same as the pattern line.

Check the paper pieces you have cut against accurate graph paper to make sure corners are square, and that 45-degree diagonals cross the intersections of the graph lines when one point is placed at an intersection. The traced pieces should fit together to make a block exactly 10" square. If they do not, you will need to adjust the size or even redraft the pattern (see the lecture in this lesson) before marking your fabric.

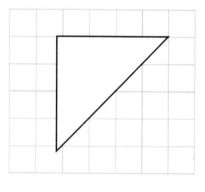

ALWAYS CHECK PATTERNS AND TEMPLATES BEFORE USING THEM!

Printing processes can distort the shapes; avoid disappointment by measuring carefully.

Transfer the paper patterns accurately to your template material by marking around it. Use a ruler to keep the edges straight, and use a sharp pencil or pen with a fine point.

Cut the templates as accurately as possible. A mat knife or craft knife and a metal ruler work well for straight lines. Scissors can be used for lines of any type. After cutting the template, re-check it against the graph paper.

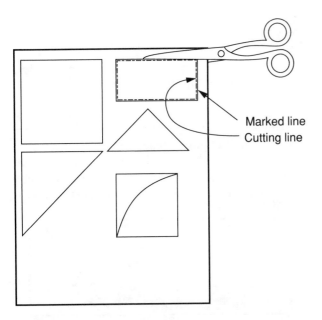

Marked line
Cutting line

Write on the template the name of the pattern, the identification letter of the piece, and the number of pieces of each fabric to cut.

All the templates for one pattern can be stored in a plastic sandwich bag to protect them and keep them together.

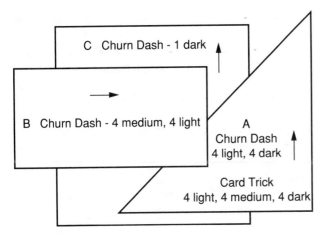

C Churn Dash - 1 dark

B Churn Dash - 4 medium, 4 light

A Churn Dash 4 light, 4 dark

Card Trick 4 light, 4 medium, 4 dark

Grain Line
You should also mark your templates with an arrow indicating the direction the *grain line* of the fabric should go.

The grain line is related to the way the fabric is woven. The *straight grain* is parallel to the sel-

vage and the *cross grain* is at right angles to it. The fabric is stable and will not stretch in these directions because the threads of the weave don't stretch. (Actually, the cross grain stretches a little bit, but not enough to worry about here.)

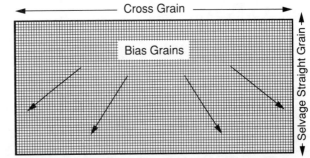

Cross Grain

Bias Grains

Selvage Straight Grain

The edge of a piece cut in any other direction will stretch and is considered *on the bias*. The general rule is: *Every piece of fabric in a block should have the grain (threads) running in the same direction, parallel to the edges of the block.*

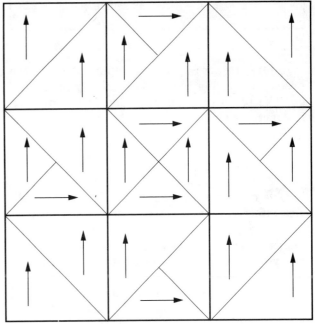

Because of this rule, you need to carefully determine which way the grain should go when you cut a triangle. If the short sides are parallel to edges of the block (often called a ½-square triangle), it should be placed on the fabric so that the short sides are parallel to the selvage. If the longest side is parallel to the edge of the block (called a ¼-square triangle), it should be parallel to the selvage when you mark your fabric.

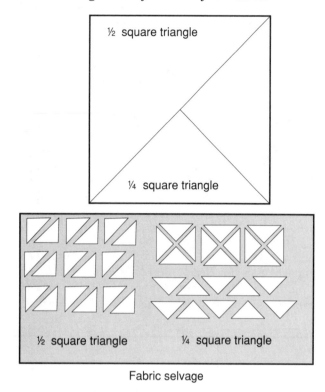

Fabric selvage

Mark an arrow on each template you have prepared showing the direction the grain should go. The block diagram included in the pattern instructions shows the normal grain line for the pieces.

Grain Line Exceptions

There are a few exceptions to this rule; they involve cutting diamonds, using the print of fabrics effectively, and constructing unusual patterns logically. We will consider diamonds in the instructions for Pattern D, the Ten-pointed Star, but you do need to think about prints at this point.

• If you are using a large or widely scattered print, you may want to center a figure in each piece you cut. If there is a right side up, such as people, animals, or landscape, or if it is a directional pattern, you need to decide whether you want it symmetrical or all going the same direction.

• If you are working with stripes, these decisions are even more critical. Stripes lead the eye just like arrows and must be planned carefully. You can place the longest edge of a triangle along a

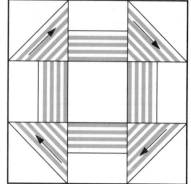

stripe, if you like, but remember that the other edges will be on a bias and stretch very easily.

• You may find that the pattern of your fabric has not been printed accurately, and you need to turn the template slightly to accommodate it. In general, the print of your fabric is more important than the grain, but again, you need to be careful not to stretch the edges while you are stitching.

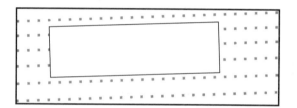

• You may also need to adjust the position of a template with prints which look like small all-over patterns, but are really off-grain stripes. Pin-dots are a good example. Line an edge of the template up with the selvage, and you will minimize problems.

• Some patterns are logically constructed with the edges of the block on the bias, such as Roman Stripe. Strips cut the length of the fabric would be stitched together, then triangles cut from them with the long sides parallel to the strips. As above, the edges would have to be handled carefully to avoid stretching.

• If your fabric has been washed and you didn't distort it when you ironed it, the fibers are as close to right angles as they will get. Fabrics which have a no-iron or permanent press finish have been heat set, and the fibers will not change position no matter how much you tug. If the grain is very uneven you can try pulling diagonally, but don't expect too much. If the fibers are *not* at right angles, you will not be able to line up all the edges of templates with the grain. If you are working with such a fabric, it is better to line up the edges of the pattern pieces with the selvage grain, rather than the cross grain.

Marking and Cutting Fabric

If your fabric was ripped by the fabric store, cut off any damaged areas. One problem with ripping is that if the threads are pulled, they may show in the fabric along the torn edge. Be sure to examine your fabric for this and don't use the damaged fabric in your blocks. Cut off the selvages so you aren't tempted to use them.

All marking for piecing is done on the *wrong* side of the fabric. If you've made a marking board, lay your fabric on it so it won't slip under the templates.

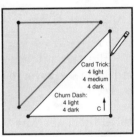

Place the template on the *wrong* side of the fabric. Make a dot at each point or corner, then connect the lines. Be careful not to distort your fabric as you mark.

Use whatever marker will give you a clear accurate line. A fine-lead mechanical pencil won't need continuous sharpening, but if the marking line doesn't show you will need a colored or washout pencil. Be sure to sharpen it frequently.

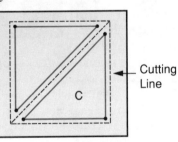

ADD SEAM ALLOWANCE

Add seam allowance before cutting out the piece. Marking around the template will give you the *seam line* for each piece. You must *add* a ¼" seam allowance for each shape to be cut, which means there will be ½" between adjacent pieces. You can use a ruler or other marker to measure the seam allowance, or you can estimate it by eye. If you normally match raw edges for accuracy, I would suggest you measure and mark the seam allowance.

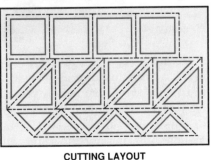

CUTTING LAYOUT

Mark all the pieces you will need of one fabric so that you are as economical of fabric and cutting time as pos-sible. Cutting lines may join each other, but do not cut more than one layer of fabric at a time unless the instructions suggest it.

Make a layout aid from a 15" square of scrap fabric, flannel or freezer paper. Pin the pieces to the layout in the right order as you cut them, right side up. You may have to overlap edges to fit them on, but it will help you stitch the pieces together correctly.

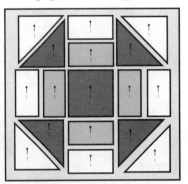

Stitching

Pin the seam lines. Match the seam lines of two pieces to be stitched together, *right sides together*. Put a pin though the top piece at the dot you made at the corner, coming out at the dot of the bottom piece. Fasten the pin at right angles to the seam. Do the same at the other end of the seam. Place pins along the seam every 2" or so, inserting the pin on the top seam line and coming out on the bottom seam line. See Illustration 3-1.

Illustration 3-1: Pinning for hand piecing.

Stitch the pinned seam. Use a fairly short (18" to 24") piece of single thread and make a small knot in it. The thread color should match the fabric if possible, but if the two pieces are different, find a color that will blend with both. (Sometimes a gray in the correct value is the best choice.)

Take a tiny stitch right over the pin in the corner. Do not stitch from edge to edge through

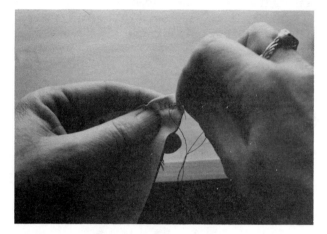

Illustration 3-2: Beginning the stitch.

the seam allowance.

Take out the pin and take another small stitch through the dots.

Take a comfortable number of small running stitches on the needle (3 to 5), checking to make sure you are on the seam line on both sides, and then pull the needle through.

When you put the needle in again, go back one stitch to start, so that you make one back-stitch with each needle full of running stitches. You should take at least 10 to 12 stitches per

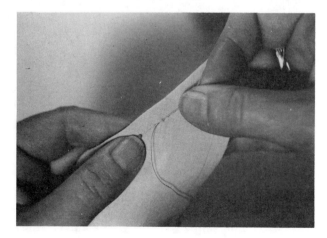

Illustration 3-3: Taking a backstitch.

inch, and more if you can.

End with a backstitch or knot. You might like to try the "Neat Knot." Take a very small stitch, and then pass the thread at the eye under the

point of the needle in one direction, and the thread from the stitch under the point in the other direction. Pull tight.

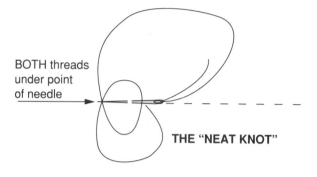

BOTH threads under point of needle →

THE "NEAT KNOT"

Pin the stitched pieces back onto the layout aid to make sure you have sewed them together correctly.

To stitch units of squares rows together, pin them the same way you did the individual pieces, putting the pins first in the corners, then along the seam lines. If there is a seam to cross, put the pin through the corner dot and the matching seam line. *Do not pin or stitch down the seam allowance.*

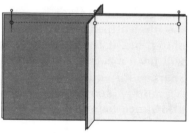

When you reach the seam, take a backstitch though the corner dot. Put the needle in through that dot, through the dot on the back seam allowance (if any), and back out at the adjacent dot. Make a backstitch through that dot; then continue stitching.

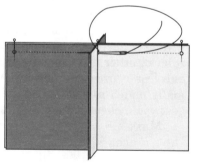

Pressing

Do as much stitching as you can before pressing, but do not stitch across any unpressed seam. Be careful not to *distort the fabric* when you press, especially bias edges. Don't pull on the edges of the pieces, or push the fabric with the iron. "Pressing" means to flatten out the seams with the heat and the weight of the iron.

Press the seams together first, to "set" the stitching.

Then press the seams toward the darker fabric so a shadow won't show from the top.

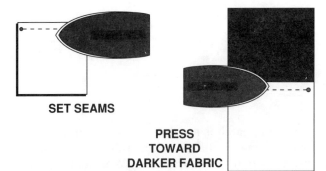

SET SEAMS

PRESS TOWARD DARKER FABRIC

Be consistent about which way you press the seams. You may change your mind about which direction they should go after you decide where you will quilt. This is one reason you don't stitch through seam allowances, so you can always press the seams in a different direction.

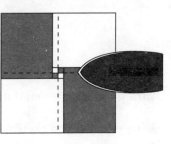

If a number of seams meet at a corner, you may need to press them all in the same direction (clockwise or counterclockwise) to reduce bulk. Construction, for instance in curved pieces, may also dictate the direction the seam is pressed. Make sure that the edge of a darker fabric does not show through the lighter; trim it back if that happens.

If you don't have access to an iron (at a meeting, for instance) you can temporarily finger-press a seam by running your thumbnail down it, but be very careful not to pull and distort the fabric.

The finished block should be pressed right side up on a folded thick towel.

Sequence of Stitching

Block designs which are based on square subdivisions are put together by first stitching square units, then making rows, and finally stitching the rows together. The instructions for each pattern give detailed sequence directions.

When you have completed all the square units and pinned them back on the layout, check to make sure that the design still looks the way you planned it. As you sew, be careful to put the correct edges of the squares together, or you may unintentionally end up with an "original" design.

Quilting

A suggested quilting design is indicated on the instructions for each block pattern. However, you may quilt the blocks any way you wish. Follow the instructions in Lesson One for basting the completed block to the batting and backing and for quilting it. Use the same color thread for quilting that you are using for the all-quilted blocks, or select one to match or contrast with your fabrics.

> *Note: Although the background blocks you cut have a ½" seam allowance, your pieced block has only a ¼" seam allowance. Don't worry if the pieced and quilted blocks are not the same measurement; we'll take care of that later. Match the corners of the pieced blocks to the center of the edge of the batting and backing blocks; then baste as directed in the General Instructions.*

Pattern A: **Churn Dash**, *Beginner Level*

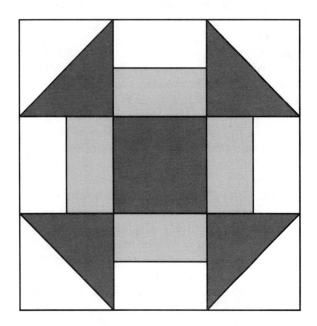

This nine-patch is a simple block design, and has many names in different localities. Some of them are Sherman's March, Monkey Wrench, Swallow, Dragon's Head, and Greek Cross.

STEP 1:

Construct templates according to the General Instructions from pieces A, B and C on page 61.

Be sure to check the patterns and the finished templates for accuracy. You only need one template of each shape, even though you will be cutting more than one fabric with some of them.

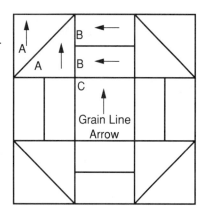

Label the templates with the name of the block, the letter of the pattern piece, the number of pieces to cut of each color, and the arrow for the grain line.

STEP 2:

Mark the templates on the fabric.

Using your colored sketch, follow the General Instructions on page 48 to mark around the templates on the fabric. Remember to mark the *wrong* side of the fabric, and remember that marking around the template will give you the *seam line* for each piece. Be sure to add a ¼" seam allowance around each piece when you cut it out. Mark pieces so that their cutting lines are right next to each other to save fabric and time.

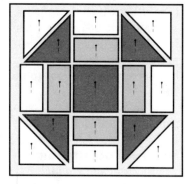

As each group of pieces is cut, fasten them to the layout backing as described in the General Instructions.

STEP 3:

Stitch pieces together in the following sequence, following the General Instructions:

a: Stitch corner "A" triangles together to make squares. Be sure you stitch the correct edges together and be careful not to stretch the bias. Press and pin them to the layout backing.

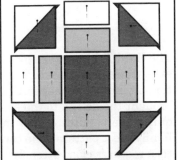

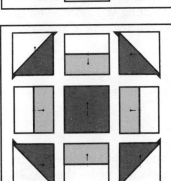

b: Stitch "B" rectangles together to make squares. Press and pin them to the layout backing.

STEP 4:

Stitch rows together.

a: Unpin Square 1 from layout backing and place it, right side down, on Square 2. Temporarily pin the seam you will be sewing to make sure you stitch the correct edges together. Unpin Square 2 from the backing and re-pin the seam accurately. Stitch the seam, referring to the General Instructions for crossing a seam.

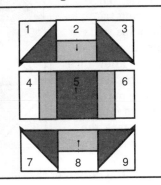

b: Lay the seamed squares over Square 3 and follow the same steps. Press and pin back to the layout backing.

c: Do the same with 4-5-6 and 7-8-9.

STEP 5:

Stitch rows together.

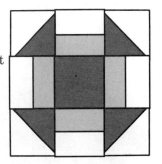

a: Unpin Row 1 and lay it right side down over Row 2. Pin the seam temporarily. Unpin Row 2 and re-pin the seam accurately. Stitch.

b: Stitch the seamed rows to Row 3 in the same manner. Press seams.

IMPORTANT! Piecing must be accurate where the seams cross. Be sure they meet exactly! If one piece is slightly larger than the other, ease the fullness in. *Do not stitch through seam allowances!*

STEP 6:

Press the block according to the General Instructions. Baste to the batting and backing and quilt.

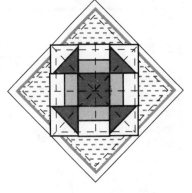

Suggested quilting design

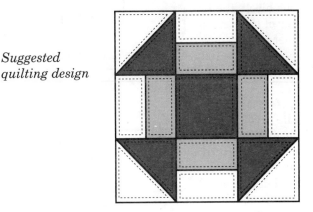

Pattern B: **Card Trick,** *Intermediate Level*

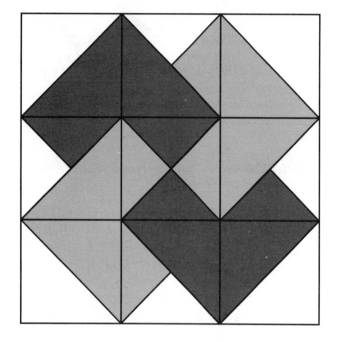

The Card Trick pattern looks very complex and even three-dimensional, but it is based on traditional nine-patch shapes. Jeffrey Gutcheon brought the design to the attention of modern quiltmakers, but it is also an ancient Japanese family crest pattern. The complexity of the pattern requires close attention to the cutting and stitching sequence, even though the shapes themselves are simple and familiar.

STEP 1:

Using the pattern on page 61, prepare accurate templates for A and D, according to the General Instructions. Label the templates with the name of the block, the letter of the pattern piece, and number of pieces to be cut.

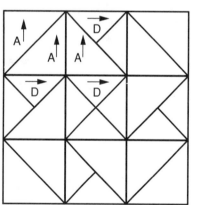

Alternate Grain Lines

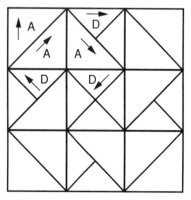

Before marking the arrow for the grain line, analyze the pattern and your fabric and decide which way it should go for each piece. The first choice would be the first

diagram, but if you are using a striped fabric, you may want to use the second diagram. In either case, triangle D on the outside edge of the block should have the longest edge on the straight grain.

STEP 2:

Mark and cut the fabric. When piecing triangles, it helps to have an accurate ¼" seam allowance. Use a ruler or other marking tool to measure and mark the seam allowance.

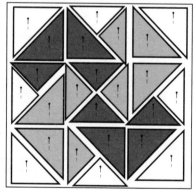

Since the design of this block is complex and mistakes are easy to make, I would suggest cutting the background pieces which go around the edges first. Pin them to the layout fabric. Then cut the pieces for each color and pin them in place as you go. Be sure to follow the grain lines marked on the templates when you place them on the fabric.

STEP 3:

Stitch the pieces in the following sequence, using the stitching directions in the General Instructions:

a: Stitch the corner squares first. Press and re-pin to the layout fabric.

b: For the middle squares on the edges, stitch the two small triangles together first. Check to make sure you are stitching the correct edges together. Press.

c: Stitch them to the large triangle, which will NOT be the same color. Do not stitch through the seam allowance. Press the seam toward the large triangle and re-pin to the layout fabric.

d: Stitch the remaining small triangles together for the center square. Be sure the colors are in the right position

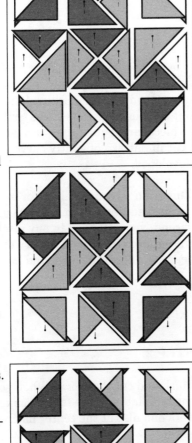

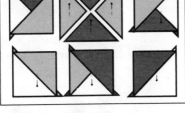

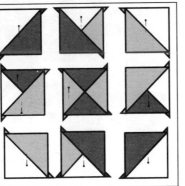

as you work, and that the seams cross exactly in the middle. Press all seams in the same direc-

tion, fanning them at the center. Re-pin all to the layout fabric.

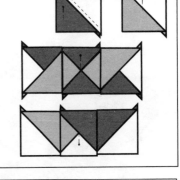

STEP 4:

Stitch the squares into rows as in Pattern A, STEP 4.

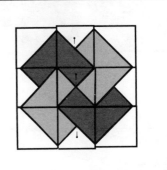

STEP 5:

Stitch the rows together as in Pattern A, STEP 5.

IMPORTANT! Piecing must be accurate where the seams cross. Be sure they meet exactly! If one piece is slightly larger than the other, ease the fullness in. *Do not stitch through seam allowances!*

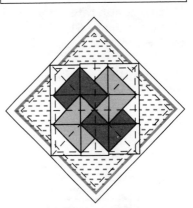

STEP 6:

Press the entire block according to the General Instructions. Baste to the backing and batting and quilt.

Suggested quilting design

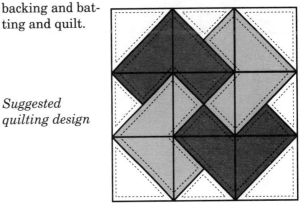

Pattern C: **Bud Bouquet**, *Advanced Level*

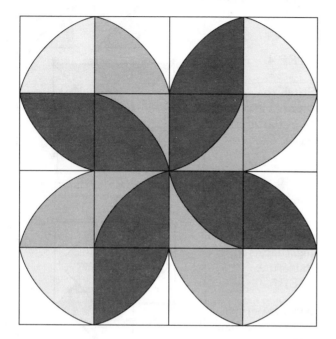

The basic shape for this pattern is a modern variation of the traditional "Drunkard's Path" pattern (developed by Joyce Schlotzhauer). She smoothed out the quarter-circle curve so it would be easier to piece, and ended the curve at the corners so an overall pattern of gently curved lines could be developed.

This is an advanced block for two reasons: first, the curved lines are more difficult to piece; and second, you will need to pay attention to piecing the squares together. It's very easy to stitch a seam on the wrong edge and have to rip it out.

STEP 1:

Construct accurate templates from pattern pieces E and F on page 61, following directions in the General Instructions.

Before cutting out the template pieces, be sure to mark the center of the curved seam on both pieces. Cut them carefully so the points on the outer circle are accurate. Test them for accuracy before using them.

Grain Line Arrows

STEP 2:

Mark and cut the fabric. When you mark around the templates on the fabric, make dots at the corners and also at the center notch of the curved seams.

The seam allowance on the curved seams should be slightly smaller than ¼" for ease in piecing. Pin the pieces in the correct order to a layout backing.

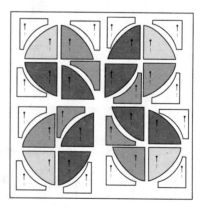

Hint:
Do not clip any curves, since it will be difficult to get a smooth line if you do.

STEP 3:

Stitch the squares together.

a: Holding the two pieces for a square (inner and outer circle), right sides together with the inner circle facing you, insert a pin in the center dot, and out through the center dot in the outer circle seam.

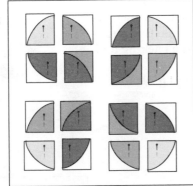

Illustration 3-4: The first pin for a curved seam

Even up the "ears" and fasten the pin. See Illustration 3-4. Then insert a pin in the dot at the left corner of both pieces. Fasten on the seam line. See Illustration 3-5.

Illustration 3-5: Adding pins to the curved seams

b: Temporarily place a pin through the corner dots at the right corner while you pick up your needle. Don't fasten the pin; just take a back-stitch over it to hold the corner and then remove it. See Illustration 3-6.

Illustration 3-6: Beginning the curved seam

c: With the inner circle still facing you, curve the two pieces slightly around the thumb of your left hand and adjust them so the seam lines match. Check the back frequently as you stitch, to make sure you are on the seam line with your needle. See Illustration 3-7.

Illustration 3-7: Continuing the stitching

d: Press the seam towards the inner circle. If the outer circle fabric is darker and the seam shadows through, trim it back. Pin the completed square to the layout backing.

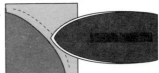

STEP 4:

Stitch the completed squares together in the following sequence:

a: This is where you need to be careful. Stitch four squares together into four-patches. All of the seams at the center should be pressed in the same direction, like a pinwheel, so the seam allowances will lie flat.

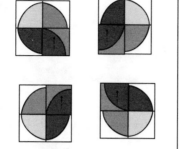

IMPORTANT! Piecing must be accurate where the seams cross. Be sure the seams meet exactly! If one piece is slightly larger than the other, ease the fullness in. *Do not stitch through seam allowances!*

b: Stitch the four-patches together. Do not stitch down the seam allowances. Press seams at the center in the same direction as above.

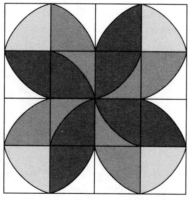

STEP 5:

Press the completed block as directed in the General Instructions. Baste to the backing and batting and quilt.

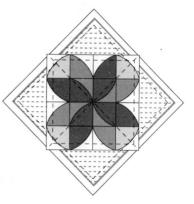

Suggested quilting design

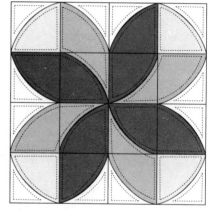

TEMPLATE PATTERNS

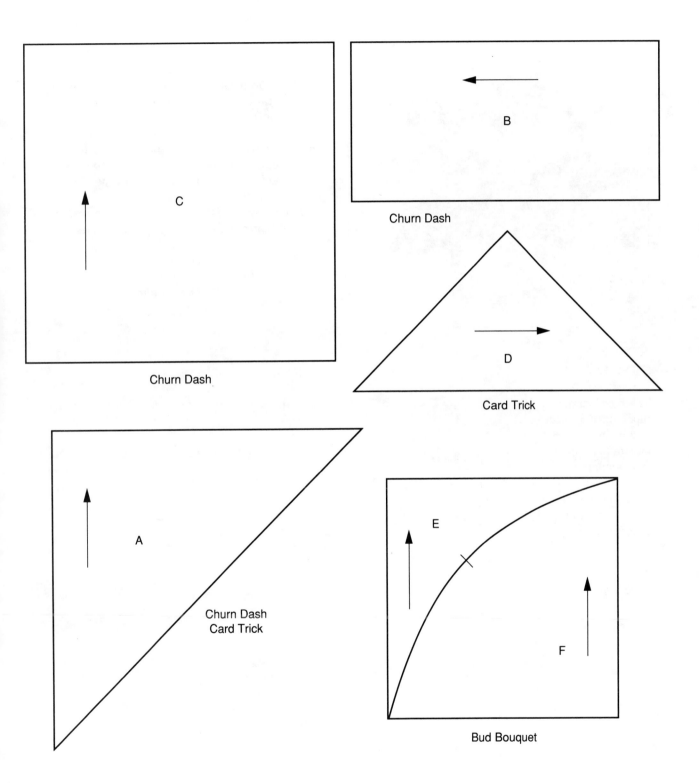

Churn Dash

C

Churn Dash

B

Card Trick

D

A

Churn Dash
Card Trick

E

F

Bud Bouquet

Pattern D: **Ten-Pointed Star**, *Challenge Level*

This block is constructed using freezer paper as a modification of the "English" paper piecing technique. Stabilizing fabric with paper is an easy way to control the unusual angles of the star points. Normally the paper pieces would be cut from typing-weight paper; then the fabric shapes would be basted over the edges, but I have eliminated the basting by taking advantage of the plastic coating on freezer paper.

> *Note: If you wish to use plain paper instead of freezer paper, cut paper pieces as directed in STEP 1, and then, instead of ironing the edges of the fabric in STEP 3, turn them over the paper by hand and baste with long stitches.*

STEP 1:

Trace the complete block pattern accurately on the dull side of a 12" piece of freezer paper. Add grain line arrows to each piece. Cut the pieces apart as accurately as possible.

STEP 2:

Cut the fabric pieces. One advantage to the paper-piecing method is that you can cut as many layers of fabric at a time as your scissors will handle. Just fold the fabric to the number of layers required (five of each fabric if you want the overlapping effect). Pin one of the paper shapes to the top layer and cut with a generous ¼" to ⅜" seam allowance. Remember to reverse corner pieces G and H.

STEP 3:

Turn and press the edges of the fabric over the paper templates.

Lay a piece of fabric wrong side up on the ironing board; then pin a freezer paper piece shiny side up on top of it. Carefully use the iron to press the seam allowances over the paper shape. Be sure the fabric is folded right at the edge of the paper, particularly at the sharp point of the diamond.

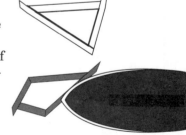

Don't try to fold in the seam allowances at the points; they won't be in the way when you stitch.

It won't hurt the tip of your iron if it gets on the freezer paper, but don't run it any farther in than necessary. Be sure the fabric is firmly adhered to the paper.

Do not press the seam allowances for the outside

edges of the block over the freezer paper.

Pin the prepared pieces to the layout.

STEP 4:

Stitch the prepared pieces in the following sequence:

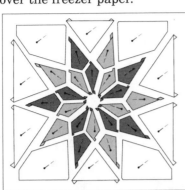

a: Pin two small diamonds with the right sides of the fabric together, edges to be joined matching. Use an applique needle and a single thread. Knot the end, and then take a stitch which catches a thread of both folds, about ⅛" from the point. Stitching toward the point, take tiny whip stitches close together until you get exactly to the point fold; then work back along the seam to the end. Do not stitch through the excess seam allowances at the points, but you may fold them back out of the way. It is vital to be accurate at the center.

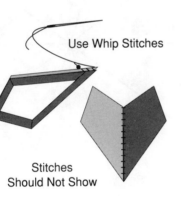

Use Whip Stitches

Stitches Should Not Show

Open up the two pieces and check the seam. The stitches should not show. If they do, you are taking up too much of the fold with the whip stitch.

b: Stitch a large diamond between the two small diamonds.

To set in the large diamond, it will be necessary to fold one of the small diamonds

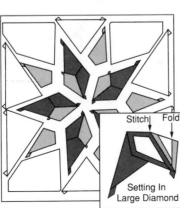

Stitch Fold

Setting In Large Diamond

so the seams will match. Always stitch from the center to the outer edge.

c: Stitch small diamonds together until the center star is completed.

d: Add the remaining small diamonds.

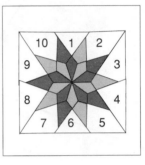

e: Set in the outside pieces, in the sequence shown.

```
10  1   2
9       3
8       4
  7  6  5
```

STEP 5:

Turn the block over and gently pull the seam allowances of the fabric off the freezer paper and remove the paper. If desired, trim the bulk of the center seams a little. BE CAREFUL! Press the seams lightly, then baste to the backing and batting and quilt.

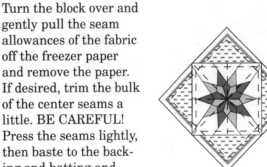

Suggested quilting design

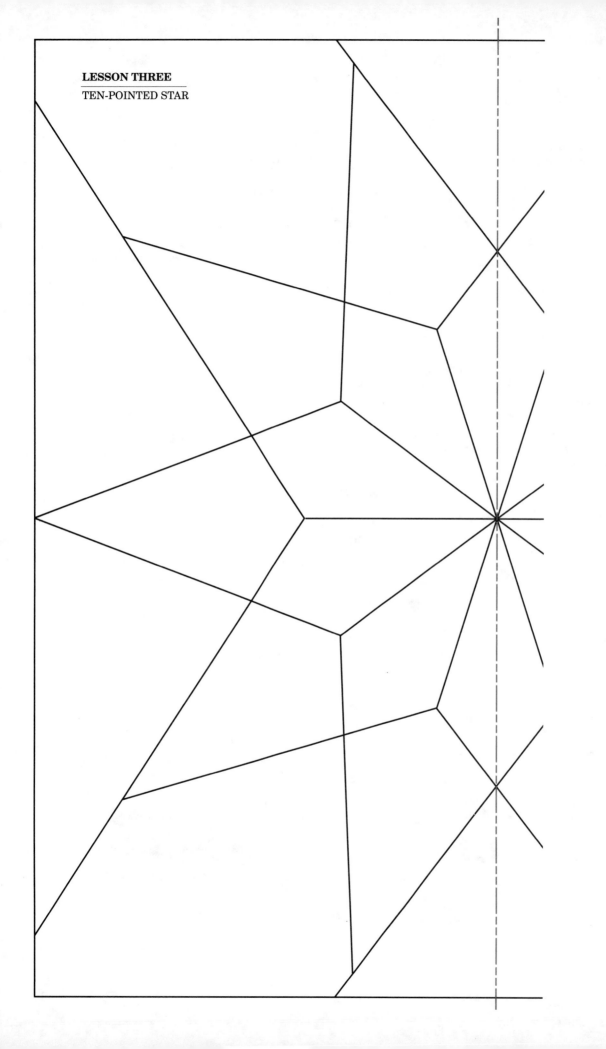

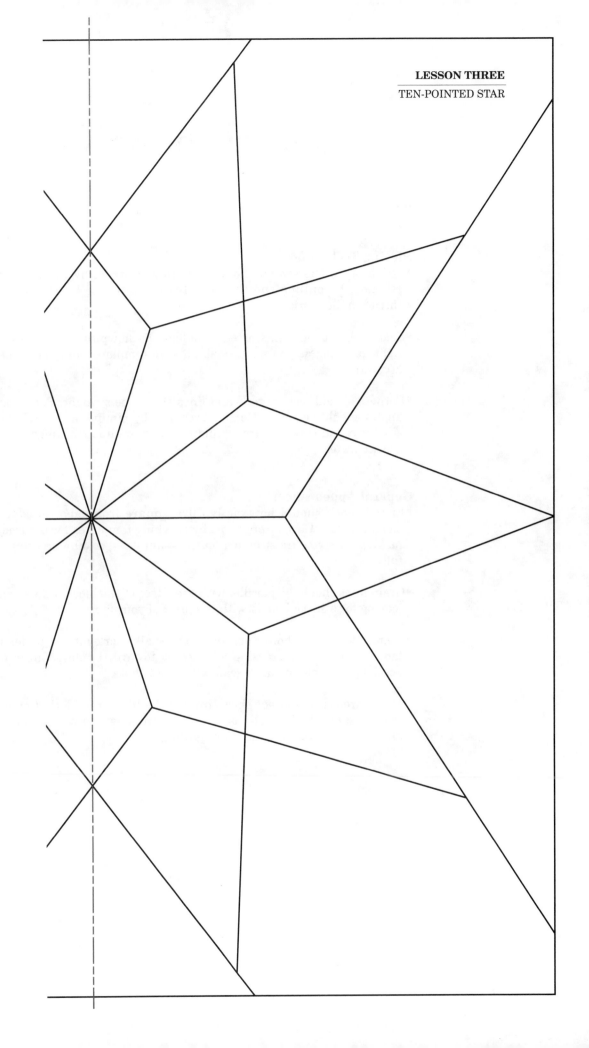

HOW ARE YOU DOING?

When you have finished your blocks, check them to see how well you are doing.

Piecing Technique:

• Stitching in the seams should not show. Correct by taking smaller stitches, by pulling the thread a little tighter, or by matching the thread to the fabric.

• Seams should lie flat. Correct problems by not pulling the thread as tight, pressing as you go, or making sure templates and markings are accurate.

• Corners should meet *exactly* and lines should be straight. Points on triangles should be sharp. Correct problems by pinning accurately before stitching, and making sure templates and seam line markings on fabric are accurate.

General Appearance:

• Pieced block should be exactly 10½" square from edge to edge and should lie flat. Correct problems by checking templates for accuracy, by making sure you are stitching on the seam lines, and by pressing carefully.

• Grain lines should be parallel with the edges of the block unless you are looking for a special effect with the print of your fabric.

• Seam allowances should not show, especially dark fabrics under light fabrics. Correct by pressing allowances toward the dark fabric when possible, or trimming dark seam allowances back.

• Stray threads should not show through the top of the block. Correct by trimming off all the "schnibbles" (loose threads and corners of triangles) before basting the block for quilting.

LECTURE: DRAFTING PIECED BLOCKS

Drafting Pieced Blocks

Learning to draft your own patterns is an important skill if you decide to continue making quilts. It frees you to make a quilt from any pattern you admire in a picture or see at a quilt show, allows you to adjust the size of a block to fit evenly into any design or any size quilt, and to redraft inaccurate patterns you have found in books or magazine.

Tools Required

The best place to get the tools and supplies you need for accurate drafting is an art supply or drafting supply shop. The things you need will cost more there than they would in an office supply store, but will also be of better quality.

Ruler: An 18" cork-backed metal ruler doesn't slip on paper (or fabric) and can be used with a pen without smearing the ink.

Paper: Accurate graph paper is the most important tool for pattern drafting. It comes in square grids of 4, 8, or 10 divisions to the inch, as

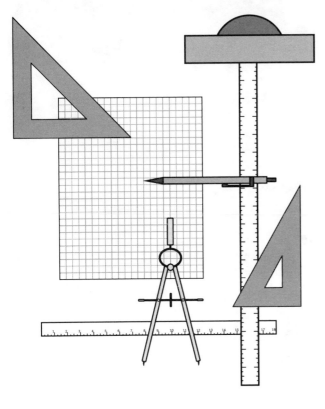

well as *isometric* grids for patterns based on hexagons and equilateral triangles.

Don't assume that even expensive graph paper is accurate enough, measure to make sure. Place the metal ruler on the paper, and note whether the markings coincide with the grid, particularly at the inch marks, and whether the grid is even both horizontally and vertically.

Pads of square graph paper are available at quilt shops, and are convenient to use, but be sure to check the accuracy.

Compass: A V-shaped compass will draw circles up to 10" in diameter; for larger circles you will need a bar compass.

Triangles: An assortment of clear plastic triangles, both right-angle and 30-60-90 degree, in large (14" or more) and small sizes, will be helpful when you begin to venture beyond the basic patterns.

T-Square and Drawing Board: If you find yourself doing much pattern drafting, these tools are a good investment to keep your lines exact.

Technical Pen with a variety of point widths: An expensive tool, but wonderful to use.

Drafting Traditional Patterns

There are two ways to approach making a geometric block pattern exactly the size you want it to be: one is to draft it to that size, using traditional methods of constructing lines and angles, the other is to use accurate graph paper divisions to draft the pattern in a convenient size, then take it to a quick printer or blueprint service to have it enlarged (or reduced) to exactly the size you want it. (If you have access to a graphics program on a computer, you can also use this method to design your block in a convenient size, then print it out and enlarge it.) Let's go through both methods, using them to draft a 10" nine-patch block.

The first step is to draw an accurate square on graph paper.

If you are going to have the pattern enlarged, you could make it 9" square, since this measurement can conveniently be divided by 3 to give the 9 squares in the block. Draw in the major divisions, then add any diagonals to make triangles, or straight lines for smaller square or rectangular subdivisions. When you take the block to be enlarged, tell them you want it exactly 10" square and they will compute the percentage of enlargement for you.

However, if you will be drafting to size, the block must be drawn 10" square. Use the metal ruler and right triangle to check each corner and the measurement of each side.

Next, each 10" side must be divided by 3 to get the 9 smaller squares. The easiest way to do this is to use the metal ruler. Place the 0" mark on one side of the square, then turn the ruler diagonally until the 12" mark is on the other side. Make a dot on the paper at the 4" and 8" marks. Use a right triangle to draw vertical lines.

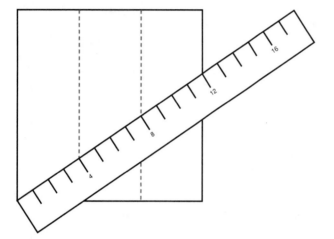

Turn the block and do the same thing in the other direction. Now the 9 squares can be subdivided into triangles with diagonal lines, or into smaller squares and rectangles, depending on the pattern. To subdivide the squares into smaller squares or rectangles, use the ruler in the same way to make equal divisions. For instance, for the Churn Dash block, you would need to divide one of the squares in half through the middle. Place the 0" mark of the ruler on one side, and 4" on the other. Make a dot on the paper at the 2" mark, then use a right triangle to make a vertical line at that point.

To draft traditional blocks based on other divisions, such as 5-patch or 7-patch, first analyze the pattern to determine the number of divisions necessary, then follow the steps which were given in this lesson to make them.

RESOURCES

Drafting your own patterns:
Patchwork Patterns and *The Quilter's Album of Blocks and Borders,* Jinny Beyer, EPM Publications, Inc., McLean, VA. You should be able to find them at quilt shops and mail-order quilt book dealers.

Mail-order drafting supplies:
Dot Pasteup Supplies, 1612 California St., Box 369, Omaha, NE 68101 ($1 for catalog).
Dick Blick, Box 1267, Galesburg, IL 61401 ($2 for catalog).

Home Study Course
in
Quiltmaking

LESSON FOUR
Traditional Applique

Pattern A: **Sunbonnet Sally**, *Beginner Level*

Pattern B: **Overall Sam**, *Intermediate Level*

Pattern C: **Traditional Tulips**, *Advanced Level*

Pattern D: **Grape Vine**, *Challenge Level*

LESSON FOUR: TRADITIONAL APPLIQUE

To use this lesson, first read its Introduction and its General Instructions. If you are making the wallhanging, decide which pattern you would like to make. Each one has the difficulty level indicated so that you can take into account your own skills, interest, and time. If you are making the full-size quilt, you will want to complete all of the blocks.

Note: If you want to construct a top and use a frame to baste and quilt, see Lesson Ten: Section Two.

INTRODUCTION TO APPLIQUE

Applique is a process of cutting out pieces of fabric, turning under the raw edges, and stitching them to a background which may be a single block or the entire quilt top. This allows a greater freedom in designing patterns than the more geometric and repetitive patterns of piecing. Applique quilts were often considered "fancy" quilts, made to be shown on special occasions or to compete for blue ribbons.

Early in American history, printed fabrics were very expensive and difficult to obtain. To make them stretch as far as possible, quiltmakers cut the figures apart and appliqued them on larger pieces of fabric so they would cover a bed. The spaces between the designs were filled in with elaborate quilting. One term used for this kind of applique is "Broderie Perse."

Later, realistic designs and recognizable forms made up of several fabrics stitched in layers were developed. Flowers, leaves, vines, children, animals, toys, and the alphabet were and are popular applique subjects. Embroidery is often used to add special touches. Pictorial quilts carry realism to the point of using the surface of the quilt as a canvas for painting with fabric for color.

The patterns in this lesson, except for the Traditional Tulips, use the quilting design in a realistic manner to enhance the subject of the block. You have already learned the effect of background grids and symmetrical designs; now you will see how the quilting line can be used to draw a picture.

RESOURCES

Big Book of Applique by Virginia Avery, Charles Scribner and Sons, New York, NY, 1978.
Chintz Quilts, Unfading Glory by Lacy Folmar Bullard and Betty Jo Shiell, Serendipity Publishers, Tallahassee, FL, 1983.
Award Winning Applique Technique by Wilma and Carolyn Johnson, American Quilter's Society, Paducah, KY, 1984.

GENERAL INSTRUCTIONS

The patterns in this lesson are given for the whole block. Trace them on graph paper as instructed in the General Instructions for Lesson Two, page 22. The solid lines are for the appliqued pieces, and the dotted lines are for the quilting design.

Making Templates

Templates for applique are made the *finished size* of the piece. Prepare them by tracing the shapes needed from the block pattern. *Do not add seam allowances to the templates.* See the instructions for each pattern for specific template directions. Mark the right side of the template with the name of the block and the piece. Store the templates for each pattern together in small plastic bags.

Preparing the Background Block

Trace around the 10" square template prepared in Lesson One, on the *right* side of a background block. Place the background block over the full-sized pattern, and *very lightly* mark the position of the applique pieces and the quilting design.

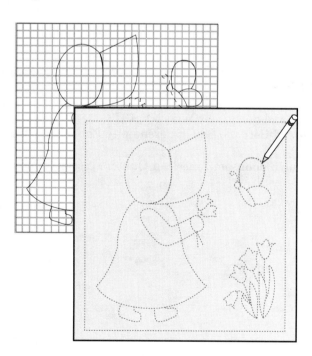

Marking The Fabric

Templates are marked on the *right side* of the fabric for applique. *Be sure the template is right side up!* Pieces should be cut with a scant ¼" seam allowance unless otherwise directed.

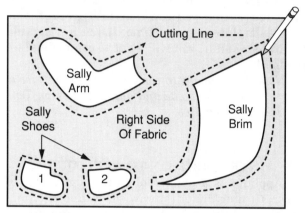

Some quilters prefer to have the grain of the pieces follow the grain of the background block. Others find they can applique more smoothly by placing as much of the edge of the pieces on the bias as possible. You should try both methods to see which works better for you. (See Lesson Three, page 49, for more information on grain lines.)

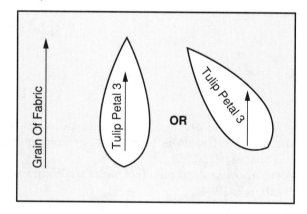

Also, if you are using fabric with stripes or a large print, remember to consider the design when you lay out the pieces.

Arranging Pieces and Basting

After you have cut out the pieces of fabric, arrange them in the proper position and sequence on the background to make sure you like the effect and that the pieces are not reversed. When you begin stitching, remove all the pieces except the one you are working on. Hold that piece in place for stitching with either pins or a thread basting ½" from the edge.

Stitching Sequence

Each applique design must be analyzed to determine the order of stitching. Stems should go under leaves, which may go under flowers, and arms and aprons go over dresses. It is important to decide the order before beginning to work, because edges that are covered by another piece should *not* be turned under. It is difficult to match two edges when both of them have been turned under. It is neater and less bulky to turn under the top edge and stitch it over the bottom piece. It is also easier to turn under an outside curve than an inside curve, and an outside curve doesn't need to be clipped, so whenever possible it should be on top.

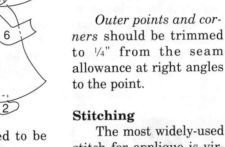

The instructions for each pattern in this lesson give you the sequence of pieces to stitch.

Preparation for Stitching

Seam allowances of each shape to be appliqued are turned under before stitching, just past the marking from the template so the marking doesn't show. There are four basic methods for turning under edges. Each pattern in this lesson will give you a chance to try one of the methods. No matter which method you use, work carefully to be sure that curves are smooth, without flat spots, and that you don't stretch any edges. Edges covered with another piece of fabric are not turned under.

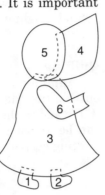

Each piece to be appliqued must be prepared before turning under the edges.

Inner curves must be clipped to prepare edges for turning. *Do not clip all the way to the seam line!* Clip very closely, about ⅛" apart, even for gentle curves.

Inner points also need to be clipped, but wait until you are ready to stitch the piece before clipping to minimize chances of the edges' becoming ragged. Clip just to the point, turn under the edges carefully, and make a couple of overcast stitches right in the point as you stitch.

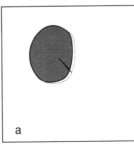

Outer points and corners should be trimmed to ¼" from the seam allowance at right angles to the point.

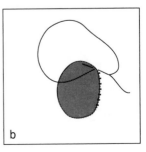

Stitching

The most widely-used stitch for applique is virtually invisible when done correctly, and holds a piece very firmly to the background. Stitching is done from the top of the block. Use regular sewing thread in a color which matches the fabric being appliqued. The thread should be about 18" long with a knot in one end.

Bring the needle up from the back of the block on the marked line for the applique, through the fold on the edges of the piece being appliqued, and take a tiny stitch through the fold. Catch only one or two threads of the fold. (a)

Reinsert the needle into the background block, right next to where it came out, parallel to the edge of the applique. Bring it back out through the edge of the fold again, about ⅛" away from the first stitch and pull the thread through, making a tiny right angle stitch over the fold. (b)

Hints:

•All of your stitches should be on the back of the background block except for the tiny stitch over the fold. As you take each stitch, give it a gentle tug, and it will almost disappear.

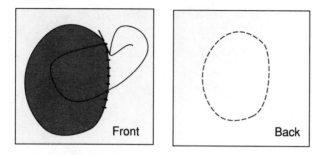

Front   Back

•Some people find that stitching in a clockwise direction with the bulk of the work away from them is easiest, while others are more comfortable and accurate stitching counter-clockwise with the bulk of the work toward them.

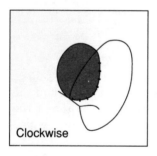 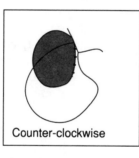

Clockwise   Counter-clockwise

Trimming

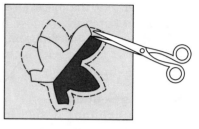

In some cases, where there are several layers of fabric or where quilting goes into the applique, the background fabric behind the applied piece should be cut away. This is the best way to prevent "shadowing," where a dark piece of fabric behind a lighter color makes the seam allowances visible.

Quilting

Applique designs should be quilted a little outside the edge of the appliqued pieces, ($\frac{1}{16}$" to $\frac{1}{8}$") to add to the three-dimensional effect. Details can be added with quilting stitches. Suggested quilting designs are included on each pattern.

Pattern A: **Sunbonnet Sally,** *Beginner Level*

This pattern is based on the popular Sunbonnet Sue patterns of the 1930's, which were favorite designs for children's quilts. It was inspired by the Sunbonnet Children stories and illustrations by Bertha Corbett.

The edges of the applique pieces in this block are turned under and basted, one of the oldest methods of prepared applique shapes. The turning was often done with an iron, but I prefer to do it with my fingers for a softer edge to the pieces.

STEP 1:

Prepare the background block according to the General Instructions, marking the applique placement and quilting design *very lightly* on the block.

STEP 2:

Make a template for each shape in the pattern, according to the General Instructions. You will need a separate template for each shape. Be sure to mark which is the right side of each template.

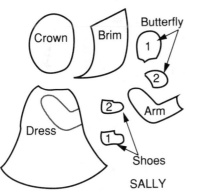

The dress shape should have the arm position indicated, but not cut out.

STEP 3:

Mark and cut the fabric pieces. Mark *very lightly* around each template on the *right* side of the fabric. Be sure the templates are *right side up* or the figure will face in the wrong direction. Add a scant ¼" seam allowance when you cut out the shapes. After you have cut the dress shape, cut the armhole out of the template and mark the position of the arm on the fabric.

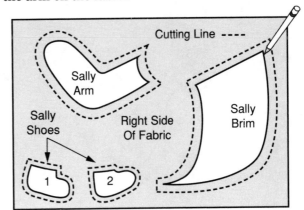

STEP 4:

Clip the inside curve of the arm, shoes, dress and the butterfly wings. Do not clip all the way to the seam line.

Baste under the seam allowance of each piece to be appliqued. Roll the seam allowance under with your fingers and baste with small stitches very close to the 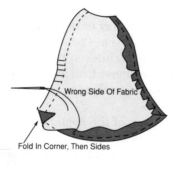 edge, making sure that the marking has been completely turned under.

Wrong Side Of Fabric

Fold In Corner, Then Sides

Do not baste under the tops of the shoes, the neckline of the dress, inside edge of the brim, or the edge of the large butterfly wing which is next to the small wing. These edges will be covered by another applique piece.

At the corners and outside points, fold the fabric at right angles to the point, then fold in the alternate sides and baste.

STEP 5:

Stitch the pieces in the following sequence, using an applique stitch as described in the General Instructions. Use a single thread the color of the piece being appliqued.

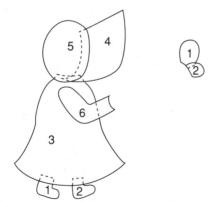

a: Pin or baste the shoes and the larger butterfly wing in position on the background block. Begin stitching at the turned edge at the top of each shoe, and at the edge of the wing.

b: Pin or baste the dress shape and the smaller butterfly wing in position, matching seam lines on the pieces with seam lines on the background block and the shoes. Begin stitching in the turned seam allowance at the neck edge.

c: Pin or baste the brim and the arm in position, matching seam lines on the piece with the background block and the dress. Begin and end stitching in the turned seam allowance at the crown edge for the brim. The entire arm shape is stitched.

d: Pin or baste the crown shape in position, matching seam lines on the piece with the background block and the brim. Stitch in place.

If any fabrics shadow through when the block is finished, trim away the background fabric.

STEP 6:

Baste the completed applique to the backing and batting. Quilt around the outside of the figure close to the edge. Quilt inside the applique around the crown, brim, and arm. Add details as indicated by the dotted lines on the pattern.

Suggested quilting design

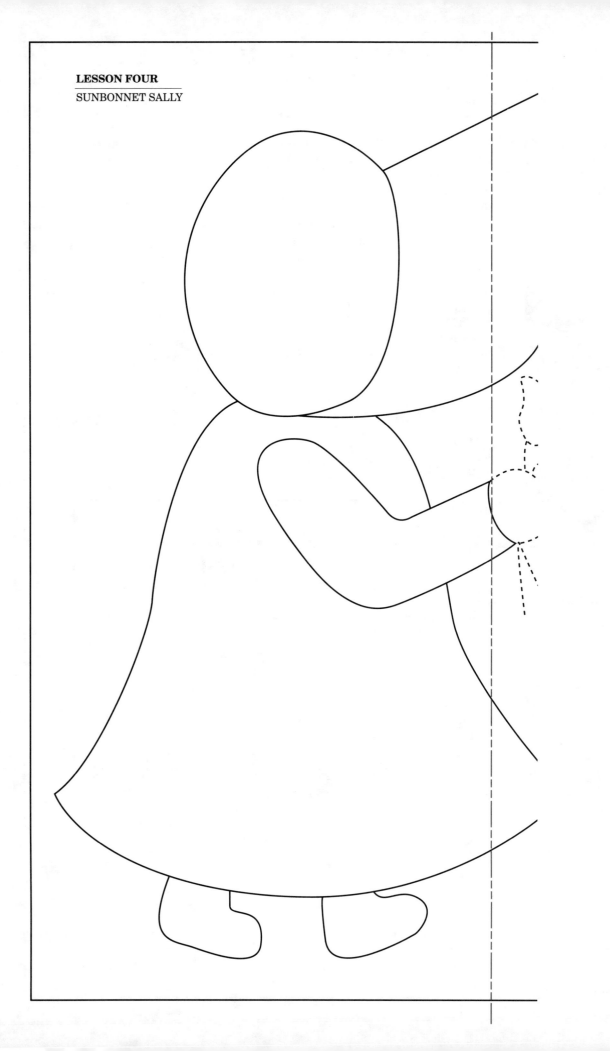

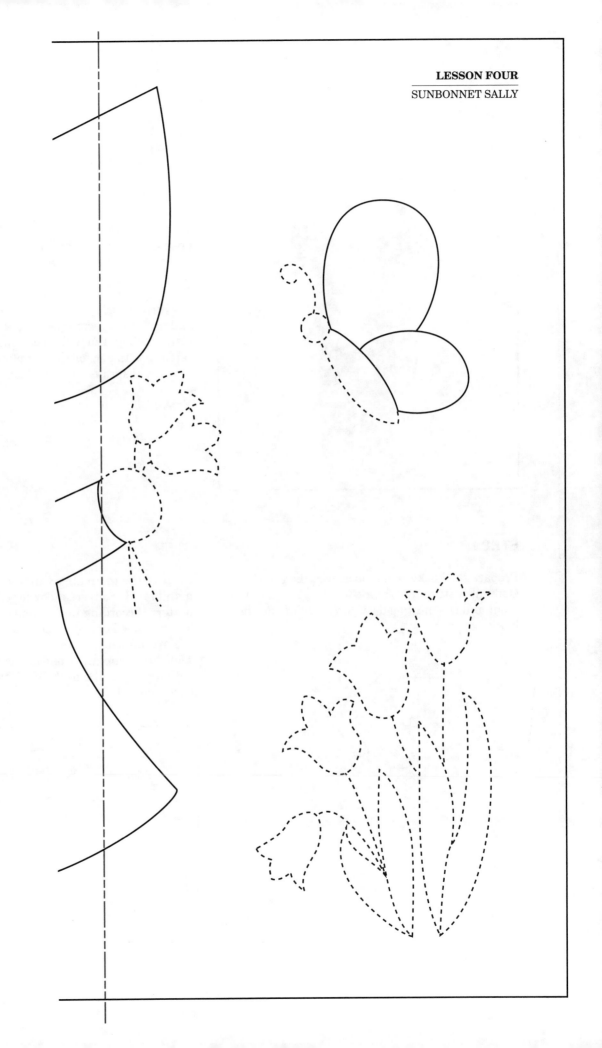

Pattern B: **Overall Sam**, *Intermediate Level*

Of course, Sunbonnet Sally had a boyfriend who helped his father in the fields while Sally was busy in the garden. Legend has it they hid behind the sunbonnet to steal a kiss.

The edges on the applique shapes in this lesson are turned under with the help of spray starch and an iron, a technique that was developed by Helen Kelley. You will need a manila folder or cereal box to use for the templates and a small amount of spray or liquid starch.

Note: If these are not available, you may use any of the other methods described in this lesson to turn under the edges on the pieces.

STEP 1:

Prepare the background block according to the General Instructions, marking the applique placement and the quilting design *very lightly* on the block.

STEP 2:

Prepare the templates. Cut a template from a manila folder or cereal box for each shape in the pattern, according to the General Instructions. You will need one for each shoe, each pant leg, the overall back, the hat crown, and the hat brim. The shirt template is one shape which includes both arms and the neck. Mark the right side of each template.

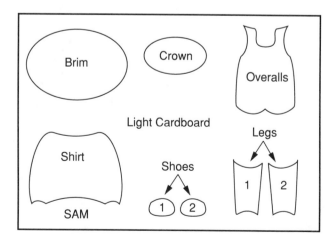

STEP 3:

Mark and cut the fabric pieces.

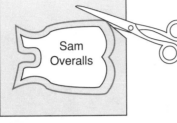

a: Lay the templates right side up on the right side of the fabric, and cut out the shapes with a generous ⅜" seam allowance. Do not mark around the template on the fabric.

b: Use the overalls template to mark *very light* seam lines on the shirt. Use the crown template to mark the position of the crown on the brim fabric piece.

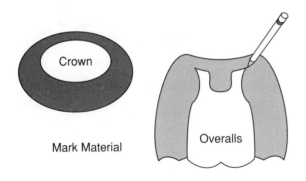

Mark Material   Overalls

c: Prepare fabric shapes for starching by clipping inside curves almost to the seam line, and clipping into the inside point of the overalls.

Clip Curves

   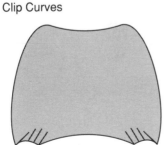

STEP 4:

Use spray starch to turn edges.

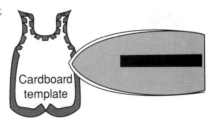

a: Protect ironing board with old pillowcase or scrap fabric. Place fabric wrong side up on board; then center template, wrong side up. *(Inside curves and points must be clipped.)* Spray a small amount of starch into a saucer or small container. Dip your finger tip into the starch and apply it to the seam allowance of the fabric, saturating it.

b: Using the tip of your iron, press the seam allowance over the template, ironing until the fabric is dry.

Remember that you should not turn under edges that will be covered by another piece. This includes the top and bottom of the pants legs, the neck and bottom edge of the shirt, and the neck edge of the overall back. Work carefully, being sure that the fabric is turned along the edge of the template and that curves are smooth.

Remove the template from the pressed fabric and trim the seam allowances to a scant ¼". Pin or baste to background.

STEP 5:

Stitch pieces to the background in the following sequence, using applique stitch as described in General Instructions. Use a single thread the color of the piece being applied.

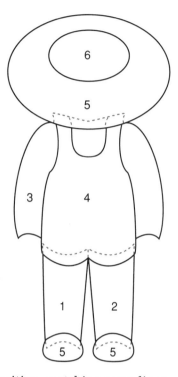

b: Pin the shirt in place. Stitch the arms only, beginning and ending in seam allowances.

a: Pin pant legs in position, matching seam lines on the piece and the background. Begin stitching in the seam allowance at the top of one leg. Slip the needle under the background fabric to continue on the second side of the leg.

c: Pin the overalls in position, matching seam lines to the shirt, background, and pant legs. Stitch in place. When you reach the inside point at the bottom of the back, make your stitches smaller and closer together to control the raw edges.

d: Pin or baste hat brim in place, matching seam lines to background block and shirt. Stitch. Pin shoes in place, matching seam lines on background and pants legs. Stitch. Pin hat crown in place, matching seam lines on brim. Stitch.

If any fabrics shadow through, trim away the background fabric.

STEP 6:

Baste the completed applique block to the backing and batting. Quilt around the figure, and inside the applique around the edge of the brim, crown, bottom of overall, and shoes. Quilt the pocket and other details as indicated by the dotted lines on the pattern.

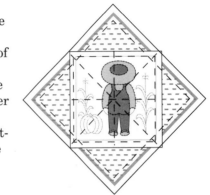

Suggested quilting design

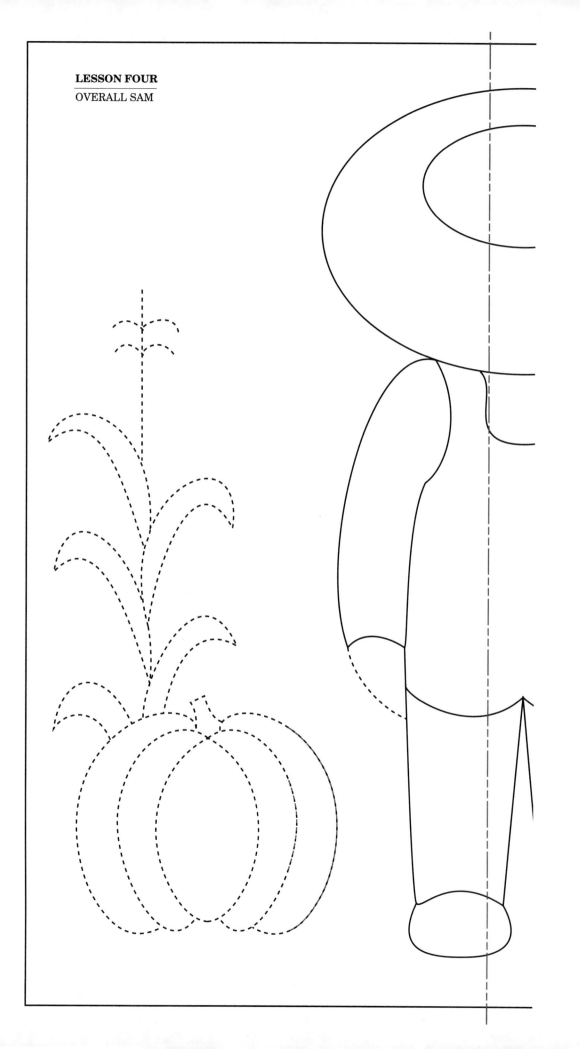

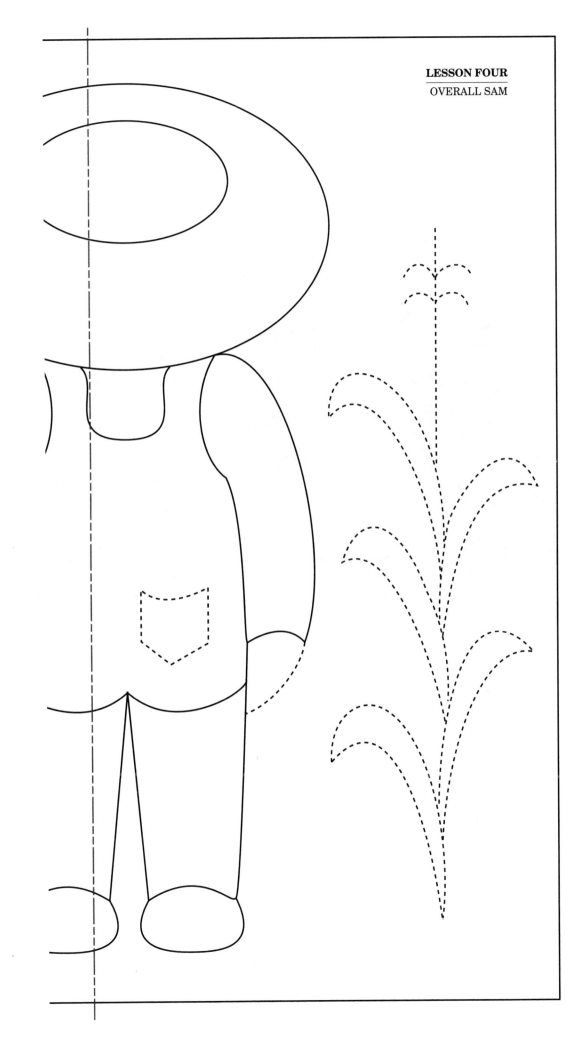

Pattern C: **Traditional Tulips**, *Advanced Level*

Flowers are favorite applique patterns, with the designs ranging from stylistic to highly realistic and natural. These tulips are reminiscent of tole painting or Pennsylvania Dutch designs.

Some of the techniques in this lesson, including the "thumb-pressing" method of turning under the applique edges, were developed by Nancy Pearson.

STEP 1:

Prepare a background block according to the General Directions.

a: To assist in placing the applique pieces correctly, fold the block diagonally into quarters and press.

b: Unfold the fabric and place it over the pattern. Trace the outside curve of the largest petal, the stems and the largest leaf shape *very lightly* on the block.

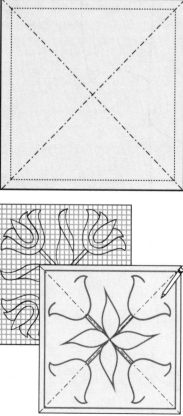

STEP 2:

Make a template for each leaf shape and each of the petals as shown in the diagram, following the General Instructions. You will not need a template for the stems. Mark a matching point at the center and ends of the overlapping leaf seam. Be sure to mark the right side of the template pieces.

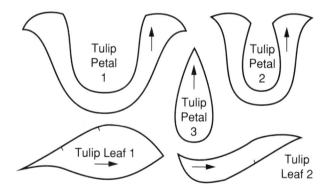

STEP 3:

Mark and cut four pieces of fabric using each shape, adding a scant ¼" seam allowance, except inside the U-shaped petals which should not be cut out. I suggest placing the grain in the longest direction of the leaf and vertical for the flower petals. Mark the matching points in the seam allowance of the larger leaf shape.

Cut two ¾"-wide pieces for the stems on the straight grain, as long as the pattern plus ½" for seam allowances.

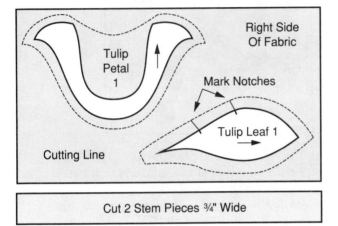

STEP 4:

Thumb-baste pieces to be appliqued. Using your thumbnail, carefully crease the edges of the pieces just inside the marked seam line before pinning or basting them in position to stitch. Be especially cautious not to stretch bias edges.

On the U-shaped petals, crease only the outer edge. At the points, crease through the seam allowance. Do not try to fold under the excess now, but use the needle to do it when you reach it in stitch-

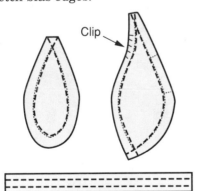

ing. Carefully clip inside curves and points of seam allowances which will be turned under. Turn under ¼" on each long edge of stem pieces and press.

STEP 5:

Stitch prepared pieces to the background block in the following sequence, using thread to match the piece being appliqued.

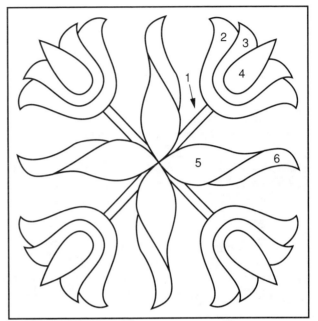

a: Fold one stem piece in half lengthwise to find the center. Match the center with the center of the background block. Pin in place along a diagonal fold. Stitch one side. Open the folds and trim the seam allowances to ⅛". Refold and stitch the second side. Repeat with second stem piece.

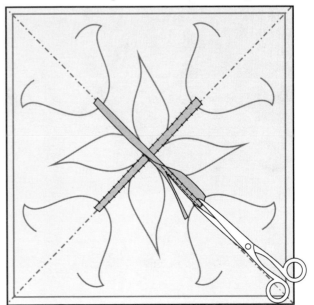

b: Pin or baste the largest U-shaped petal in place, matching seam lines with the background block. Stitch outside edges in place, clipping the seam allowance at the top.

Before reaching a point, crease a fold across the seam allowances exactly at the point the edge folds meet. Turn under the seam allowance of the point, and then the edge being stitched. At the point, take an extra stitch to hold the point in place; then take a longer visible stitch to extend the point optically. Use the needle to tuck excess fabric of the remaining edge under the piece if necessary.

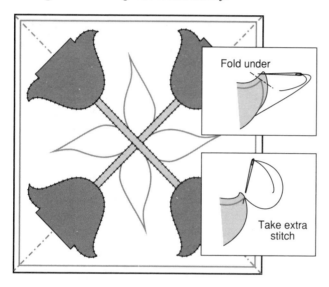

c: Place the template for the smaller U-shaped piece in position on the appliqued piece, and mark the outside edge. Trim the seam allowance of the stitched piece to ⅛". Pin or baste the smaller U-shaped petal in place, matching seam lines. Stitch the outside edges in place.

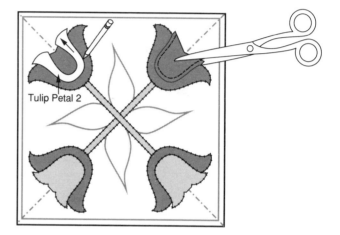

d: Place the template for the top petal over the smaller appliqued U-shape and mark the edge, and trim the seam allowance to ⅛". Pin or baste the top petal in place, matching seam lines. Stitch. Repeat steps 5b to 5d for each tulip.

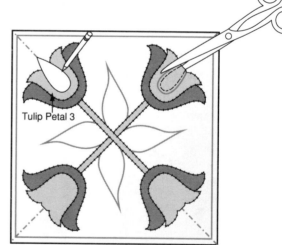

e: Place the smaller leaf-shaped template in position over the larger shape and clip to the seam allowance at the point it is covered by the top shape. Do not turn under or stitch from the clipped point to the outside edge since that seam allowance will be covered by the top piece.

Pin or baste the larger leaf shape in position, matching the lines drawn on the background block and with the wide point just over the edge of the stems. Stitch in place.

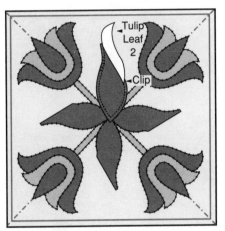

f: Place the template for the top leaf shape over the appliqued larger piece, matching the marked points, and mark the position. Pin or baste the small leaf shape into position and stitch.

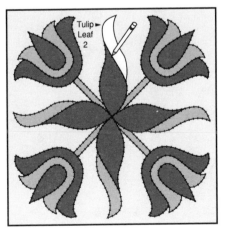

If any fabrics shadow through, carefully trim away the background fabric.

STEP 6:

Baste the completed applique block to the backing and batting. Quilt around each tulip shape, the leaves, and the stems.

Suggested quilting design

Pattern D: **Grape Vine**, *Challenge Level*

A real test of any applique needleworker's skill is how well she can do small circles and tiny bias strips. This pattern gives you an opportunity to try them. The techniques for the grapes and the vines were passed on by Carter Houck, while the needle-turning method is a modification of the Hawaiian technique used by many contemporary quiltmakers. It gives a soft edge to the applied piece.

STEP 1:

Prepare the background block according to the General Instructions, marking the edges of the leaves, the vines, the outside edges of the grape bunches and the center quilting pattern *very lightly*.

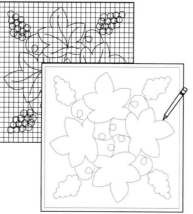

STEP 2:

Prepare a template for the leaf. Remember to mark the right side. Mark the edges where it overlaps the leaf next to it. You might want to make a stencil, as described in the lecture for this lesson.

You will need a 1" circle for the grapes. If you have something around the house or studio with that measurement (the top of a pill bottle, for instance), you may use it instead of making a template. If not, you will find it easier to mark the circles if you cut a 1" center out of a 2" square using the circle template pattern.

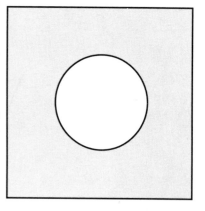

STEP 3:

Mark and cut fabric pieces.

a: Trace the leaf template on the right side of the fabric, marking the seam allowance where the overlap is. Cut out, leaving a scant ¼" seam allowance.

Mark the quilting pattern on the fabric leaf before appliqueing it.

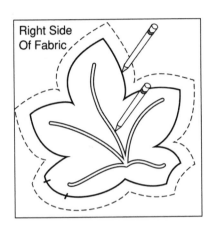

You will need 14 one-inch circles for each bunch of grapes, so mark and cut a total of 56. They may all be cut from one fabric, or you may use a variety of fabrics.

b: You will also need 24" of ¾" *true bias* strip. To find the true bias, fold the fabric you will be using on a diagonal so that the threads line up. Cut along the fold, then cut off a ¾" strip. Press the strip in half so that it is ⅜" wide. Trim the cut edge so that the folded strip is just over ¼" wide.

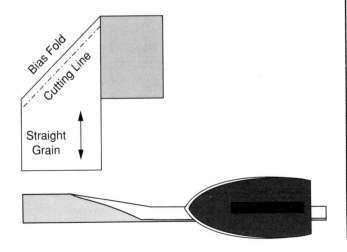

STEP 4:

Prepare the grapes for applique.

Make a knot in the end of a single thread; then run a line of very small basting stitches around the edge of a 1" circle. When you get all the way around, pull the thread tight enough for the gathers to pull in and lay flat inside the circle. If you pull the thread too tight, the gathers won't lay down. Fasten off the thread and adjust the edge of the circle with your fingers so it is smooth.

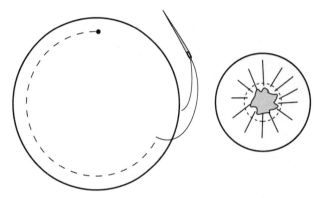

STEP 5:

Applique the pieces to the background block in the following sequence, using thread to match the piece being stitched.

a: Stitch grapes in position following the diagram below. It is not necessary to knot and cut the thread after each grape; you can run the needle behind the fabric to the next stitching position. Grapes will not lie flat; they will appear slightly stuffed.

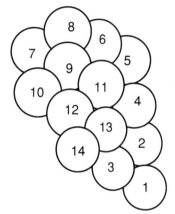

b: Applique the bias strip vines.
1) Starting ¼" inside the leaf shape, match the raw edges of the bias strip to the marked vine line and stitch. Use a running stitch a little less that half the distance between the raw and folded edges, closer to the raw edges. Be *very* careful not to stretch the bias; instead, ease the strip around the curve.

2) When you get to the point where the strip crosses itself, stop and turn the folded edge over the raw edge of the strip underneath and pin it in place. Continue the running stitch.

When you get ⅜" from the end of the marked line, carefully trim the bias on a diagonal so that the folded edge is slightly longer than the end of the line and the extra fabric triangle is on the bottom.

3) Fold the triangle into the strip and continue the running stitch, bringing it closer to the folded edge.

4) When you get to the end, take a couple of backstitches to hold the strip firmly; then carefully trim the raw edges close to the running stitches.

5) Turn the folded edge over the raw edges, stretching the bias smoothly, and applique it in position.

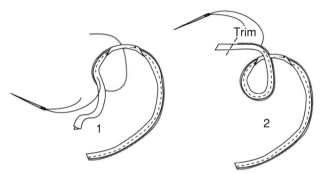

Fold Point To Inside

c: Applique the leaves.
Clip the seam allowance of the leaf shapes at the inside points. Pin or baste one to the background about ½" inside the edge.

1) Beginning at the edge of the overlap, turn a short section of the seam allowance, about 1", under with your needle. Hold it in place with your left hand and stitch the folded section down. Turn another inch and continue stitching, continuing to turn under the seam allowance just ahead of your stitching until you reach the overlap on the opposite edge.

2) At the inside points, be sure to turn under all the raw edges. The seam allowance will taper to almost nothing, so you will need to take extra stitches, almost like overcast stitches, in the point.

3) At the outside points, stitch right up to the seam line; then take a backstitch to hold it firmly while you tuck the excess fabric under with your needle.

4) Do not finish the first leaf, but fold the rest of the fabric away from the stitching line of the next leaf. The next leaf to be stitched should be the one that lies over it to the right on the pattern.

After the fourth leaf has been finished, unpin the first leaf and complete it.

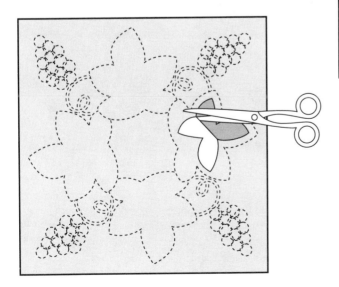

STEP 6:
When all of the leaves have been stitched, turn the block over and very carefully trim away the background, leaving a scant ¼" seam allowance.

STEP 7:

Baste the completed block to the batting and backing. Quilt around the outside of the grape bunch, but not the individual circles. Quilt around the leaves and the vines and the curls in the center. Quilt the leaf veins.

Suggested quilting design

LESSON FOUR

GRAPE VINE

HOW ARE YOUR DOING?

When you have finished your blocks, check them to see how well you are doing.

Applique stitch:
• Stitches should be close enough together that the applique is firmly attached.

• Stitching should be tight enough so that the edges of the applique lie flat.

• Stitching should not show. If the stitches are too large, take a smaller bit of the fold with the needle. Thread color should match the piece being applied.

General Appearance:
• Appliqued pieces should lie flat. If they bulge or pucker, use more pins to hold them in place while stitching, or baste them.

• Curves should be smooth. Be sure to clip inside curves closely. Use your needle to tuck under bulky spots on outside curves.

• Points should be sharp. Review the General Instructions about trimming points before stitching.

• Raw edges should not be visible. Watch inside points especially, stitching more closely to prevent raveling.

• Markings should not show, on either the background or the applied pieces. Mark with a lighter touch, or use a chalk or washout pencil which can be removed.

• There should be no shadows of dark fabrics under light ones. Trim the dark pieces if necessary.

• Circles should be smooth and round, and narrow strips should be even in width.

LECTURE: DESIGNING APPLIQUE PATTERNS

Applique is a wonderful vehicle for saving memories and expressing feelings in a visual way. Now that you have practiced some of the basic skills, you can design your own applique patterns on any theme that you wish. There are a few things to keep in mind.

Applique patterns are outline drawings of shapes. Detail may be added with quilting or embroidery stitches. If you can't draw the ideas you have, a good place to start looking for a design is children's coloring books. You can also start from photographs by tracing the outlines of the shapes and enlarging them.

One way to enlarge drawings is to work from a small grid to a larger one. For instance, if you place a ¼" grid over a small drawing (either marking it on the pattern, or using a transparent grid over the drawing), and transfer the lines in each square to a 1" grid, the finished drawing will be four times larger.

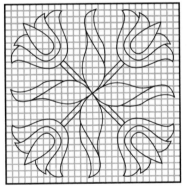

Another method is to use an overhead projector, if you have access to one, to project an image the desired size. If you tape a piece of paper on the wall behind it, you can trace the projection. A third, and the easiest and most accurate method, is to take the drawing to a blueprinting service, and tell them how big you want it. They will be able to enlarge it to the exact dimensions you specify. If the finished size is not larger than letter-size paper, many copy machines can also enlarge.

Once you have a drawing that is the right

size, analyze it to see how difficult the applique will be. Look especially at inside and outside points.

On inside points, the narrower the space between seam lines, the less fabric there will be to turn under. On firmly woven lightweight fabrics, ¹⁄₁₆" is the minimum that can be turned under without raveling; for other fabrics it

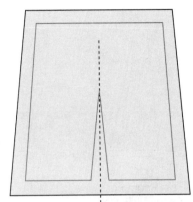
Seam Allowance Very Narrow

may be ⅛" or even ¼". When the seam allowance is narrower than that, very close applique stitches are needed to overcast the edge. There are several solutions to the problem you can try. If the pattern is suitable, divide the shape in half. If the pattern is suitable, turn the point into a small curve. Or, if the pattern is suitable, widen the angle of the point.

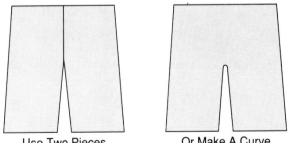
Use Two Pieces   Or Make A Curve

For an outside point, the narrower the shape is between the seam lines, the more difficult it will be to accommodate the turned-under seam allowances. Again, depending on the weight and weave of the fabric, there are limits as to how close the fabric may be trimmed to the seam line to reduce bulk. The technique, described in Pattern C, of taking a long stitch at the end of a point to serve as an optical illusion, helps somewhat. However, if you can redesign the pattern so that the point has a wider angle, it will be easier to stitch.

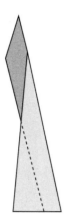 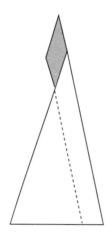

No Room For
Seam Allowance

Make Angle
Wider

Circles smaller than ½" are very difficult to stitch, since there is not enough room behind the shape to accommodate the turned-under seam allowance. However, you could use embroidery to add that kind of detail.

Parallel edges that are less than ¼" apart are also difficult to stitch for the same reason, whether they are straight or curved. With care and skill, it is possible to stitch strips as narrow as ⅛" using the method for the vines in Pattern D.

Large shapes can also be difficult to handle unless they are well basted, not only around the edges but throughout the shape. They have a tendency to become loose and puffy and not lie flat. If this happens, quilting within the shape can help control it.

Some details that would be difficult to add with traditional applique because of the problems described above can be included by using reverse applique techniques. See Lesson Seven, Patterns B and D, for more information.

Home Study Course
in
Quiltmaking

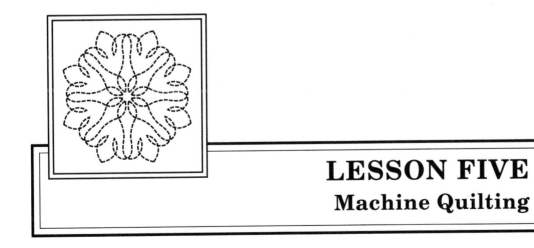

LESSON FIVE
Machine Quilting

Pattern A: **Clamshell**, *Beginner Level*

Pattern B: **Daisy**, *Intermediate Level*

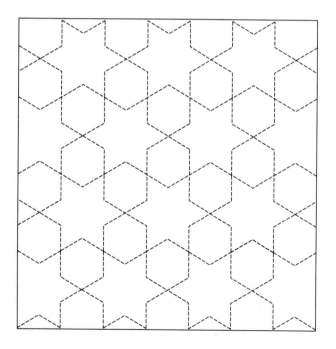

Pattern C: **Star Trail**, *Advanced Level*

Pattern D: **Tulip Wreath**, *Challenge Level*

LESSON FIVE: MACHINE QUILTING

To use this lesson, first read its Introduction and its General Instructions. If you are making the wallhanging, decide which pattern you would like to make. Each one has the difficulty level indicated so that you can take into account your own skills, interests, and time. If you are making the full-size quilt, you will want to complete all of the blocks.

Note: If you want to construct a top and use a frame to baste and quilt, see Lesson Ten; then go on to Lesson Five.

INTRODUCTION TO MACHINE PIECING

Ever since the sewing machine was invented, some quilters have used it to save time in quilt-making. They quickly learned to piece fabric together for a quilt top and to apply bindings, and when it was well done, few could tell the difference between handwork and machine work. However, doing the actual quilting with a sewing machine was slow to gain acceptance, probably because the visual effect of machine stitching is very different, but also because it is not easy to do well.

Although machine quilting is undeniably faster, it requires a lot of care in putting the three layers together and in using the machine to obtain satisfactory results. It takes practice and a good relationship with your machine. It's worth the effort to learn, though, because it adds another skill to your repertoire.

One major advantage is that since it is faster than hand stitching, pieces which are experi-

ments, which will get hard use, in which the stitching is not a design element but is needed to hold layers together (in wallhangings or clothing, for instance) can be completed and used in a much shorter period of time. Quilters with lots of ideas can get one down into fabric and finished, and then go on to the next one.

It isn't necessary to have a fancy machine or unusual equipment to machine quilt well. I have a tiny Elnita with fixed feed dogs and non-adjustable pressure on the presser foot and have been able to produce satisfactory results. My machine does have one advantage and that is a variable speed control. I wouldn't try a full-size quilt on this machine, but for single blocks or small pieces, it works well.

Not every quilting design can be used for machine stitching. The term "continuous line" is often used to describe suitable designs. They allow the path of the stitching to continue from one area to another without having to stop and break the thread, then begin again.

Most of the criteria used to evaluate hand stitching also applies to machine stitching, even though the two types of stitching don't look the same, and they are very seldom judged in the same categories.

Note: If you are frustrated or dissatisfied with your attempts to learn machine quilting, you may do the blocks in this pattern with the traditional hand-quilting process, using the techniques learned in Lesson Two.

RESOURCES

Continous Line Quilting Designs, Pat Cody, Chilton Book Company, Radnor, PA, 1984.
Heirloom Machine Quilting, Harriet Hargrove, Burdett Publications, Westminster, CA, 1987.

GENERAL INSTRUCTIONS

Adjusting Your Machine

It is a good idea to use scraps of your fabric and batting to practice stitching and adjust your machine. Cut two 10" to 12" squares of leftover fabric and a similarly-sized piece of batting. Mark some straight and curved lines and a few geometric shapes on the top fabric, and then baste around the edges. Use straight pins at right angles to the stitching lines to hold them in place.

When you begin to stitch, you may find it helpful to bring the bobbin thread to the top of the fabric so you can hold it out of the way and be sure it won't get caught on the underside.

Slowly stitch a few inches of a straight line, using a setting of 12 to 15 stitches per inch. Don't stitch over pins. If the presser foot is pushing the top fabric ahead of it and making a pleat at the pin, try one of these tactics:

• If you can adjust the pressure on the foot of your machine, decrease it.

• Hold fabric layers firmly with your fingers on either side of the presser foot, pulling your

hands slight-
ly apart. Be
careful not to
push or pull
the fabric
against the
action of the
feed dogs,
which might
bend the
needle.

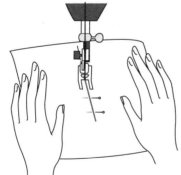

• Place pins closer together, as close as ½".

• Instead of holding fabric flat next to the presser foot, grasp it in front and back of the presser foot and pull slightly. Be very careful to let the fabric move with the feed dogs, or you will bend the needle.

• If you can drop the feed dogs on your machine, try it to see the results. The biggest problem will be getting a consistent stitch length, since the stitch length will be determined by how evenly you feed the fabric with your hands.

• If problems persist and you are determined to master the skill, purchase a darning foot (try to

find one made of clear plastic) or a walking foot for your machine.

After you have stitched a few inches, look at the stitches on the front and back closely. The bobbin thread should not show on the front, and the top thread should not show on the back. If the bobbin thread shows, loosen the stitch tension very slightly until the bottom thread disappears. If the top thread shows on the back, tighten the stitch tension slightly.

Next, try stitching one of the curved lines. It will probably take some practice to coordinate the speed of the machine and the fabric movement to make a smooth turn.

Now try some geometric shapes. When you come to a corner, leave the needle in the fabric to make the turn.

The turn should come exactly at the corner, which may require shortening the stitch length for a few stitches. After the corner is turned, return the setting to the original position.

Continue to practice stitching until you feel comfortable and have determined the best speed for the machine. Then proceed with the blocks in this lesson.

Marking the Background Block

The patterns in this lesson are given for the whole block, except for the Clamshell pattern, which is marked with a template. Trace the patterns for the other three blocks on graph paper, as instructed in the General Instructions for Lesson Two, page 22. Mark the design on the background block as directed in the pattern instructions.

Basting and Pinning for Quilting

Baste the marked block around the edges to a prepared backing block. Use straight pins to baste the stitching areas, placing them at right angles to the stitching line where possible.

Stitching

Use contrasting thread to emphasize the design, or use a thread which matches the background fabric for texture and to make stitches less visible.

Whenever possible, begin a line of machine stitching in the seam allowance of the background block. If that is not possible, you will need to hand finish the line of stitching. Be sure to leave enough thread when you start and finish a line so you can put both ends through the eye of a needle and bury them between the layers of fabric. Do not tie a visible knot in the threads on the back of the fabric as you might with other types of machine sewing.

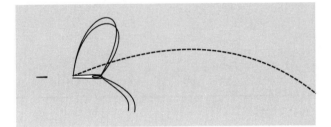

Pattern A: **Clamshell**, *Beginner Level*

The clamshell is a versatile design which is used both as a quilting grid and as a piecing or applique pattern. It is based on overlapping circles. The pattern is marked on the block using a single template.

STEP 1:

Prepare a template from the pattern, and then check it against the pattern for accuracy. It should fit just inside the lines, and be slightly less than 2" in diameter.

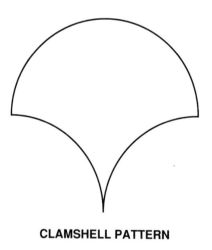

CLAMSHELL PATTERN

STEP 2:

Use the 10" template to mark the seam lines of a background block. Mark the sides of the block at 2" intervals, then press creases at the marks to assist in placing the design. (Do not use a pencil to mark the lines since they will show. However, you can use a water-soluble pencil.)

Start marking very lightly around the template on the bottom row, adjusting placement so it fits. Mark around the top curve only.

Then mark a vertical row on each side, offsetting the template by half a clamshell for the row next to the bottom and every other row. Fit the bottom curve of the template to the row below. Mark the top row.

If the marking around the edges has come out even, finish marking the rest of the block, using the pressed creases to keep the rows straight. If the marking did not come out evenly within the marked seam lines, adjust the size of the template.

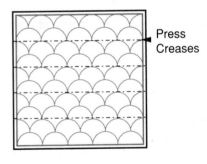

Press
Creases

STEP 3:

Baste and pin for quilting. Pin at each end of the half-circle pattern, placing pins vertically.

STEP 4:

Machine quilt, starting with the bottom row.

Subsequent pairs of rows can be stitched in one continuous line.

Pattern B: **Daisy**, *Intermediate Level*

This is a very simple pattern which can be used to develop your continuous line quilting skills.

STEP 1:

Mark the pattern on a background block.

STEP 2:

Baste and pin for quilting. Pin at the top and bottom of each petal and at each crossover of the petal edges.

STEP 3:

Machine quilt, beginning in the center of the design.

Pattern C: **Star Trail**, *Advanced Level*

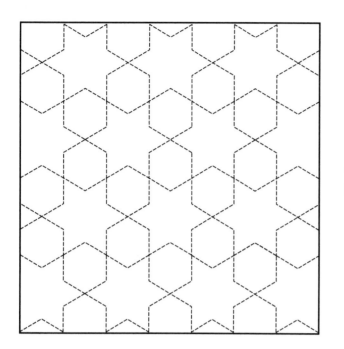

The design of this all-over six-pointed star was inspired by an Arabic geometric pattern.

STEP 1:

Mark the pattern on a background block.

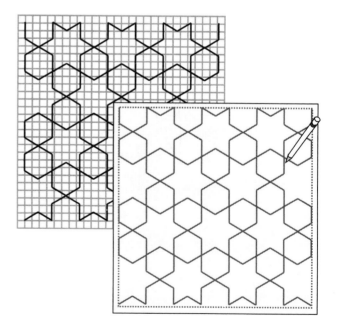

STEP 2:

Baste and pin for quilting. Pin at every intersection.

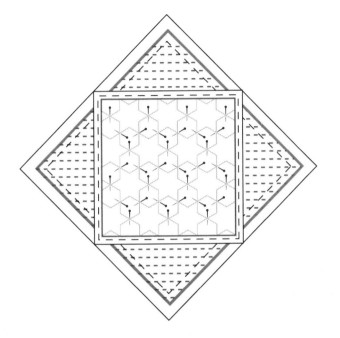

STEP 3:

Machine quilt, beginning with the horizontal lines.

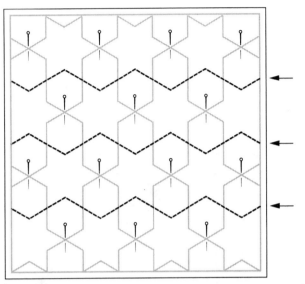

Complete by stitching the diagonal lines as shown.

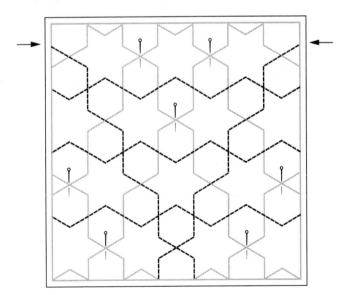

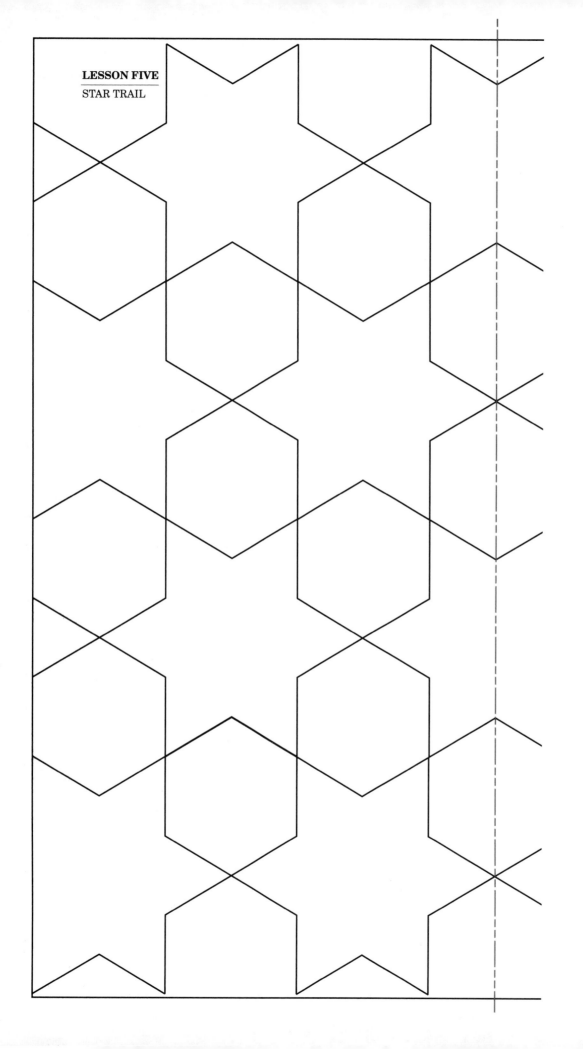

LESSON FIVE
STAR TRAIL

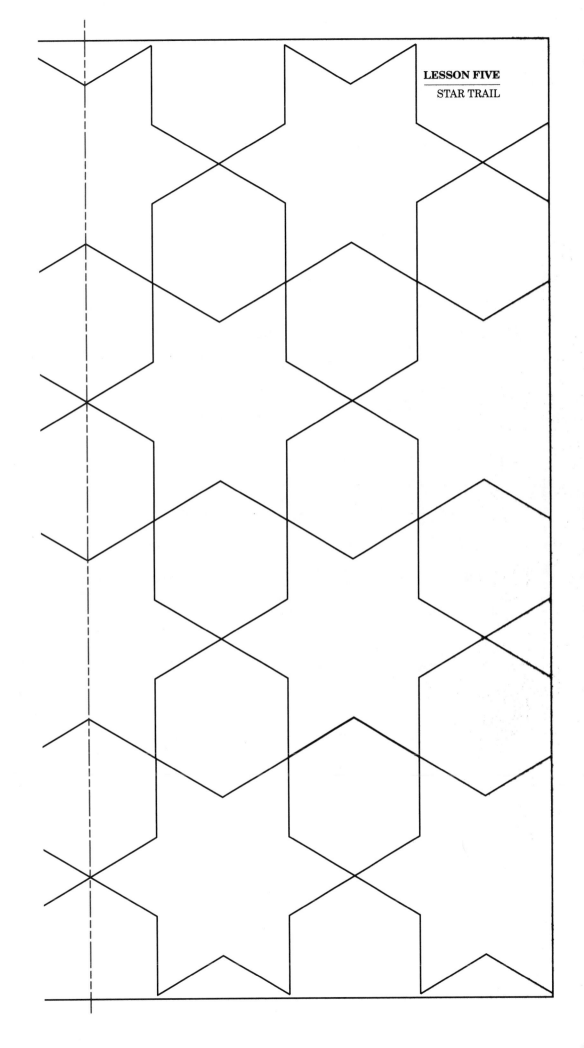

Pattern D: **Tulip Wreath**, *Challenge Level*

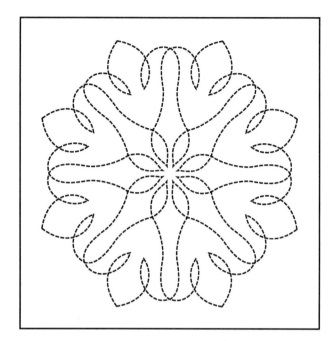

This intricate-looking pattern is done with only two lines of continuous stitching. You may want to try dropping your feed dogs or using a darning foot to negotiate the tight curves.

STEP 1:

Mark the pattern on a background block.

STEP 2:

Baste and pin for quilting. Pin at the top of each tulip, at the junctions and at the crossovers.

STEP 3:

Machine quilt, beginning at the center with the inner line.

Stitch the outer line, with contrasting thread if desired.

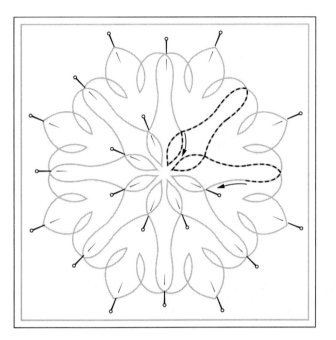

HOW ARE YOU DOING?

When you have finished your blocks, check them to see how well you are doing.

Stitching:

•Stitches should be even in size, and a length which is attractive with the fabric and batting you are using. It may take more practice to attain even stitches with a darning foot or with the feed dogs dropped.

•Corners should turn sharply. The needle should be in the fabric as the block is turned. You may need to adjust the stitch length for a shorter stitch so that the corner is precise.

•Curves should be smooth, not jagged. Stitch slowly, and watch the line you are stitching, not the needle.

•The top thread should not show in the bottom stitches, and the bottom thread should not show in the top stitches. Adjust the tension of your machine if necessary.

•The beginning and ending of the stitching line should not show. If these ends are not in the seam allowances (which will eventually be hidden), be sure to use a needle to run the ends of thread through the layers. Do not tie a knot by hand on the back, where it will show.

General Appearance:

•There should be no pleats or puckers where lines of stitching cross. Use more pins to hold the layers together along the stitching line, and use your fingers on either side of the needle to hold the fabric taut. Stitch slowly so you can control the fullness.

•The block should not be distorted by the stitching. This is particularly likely on curves. Be sure you are moving all layers as you stitch, and stitch slowly. Additional pinning will also help, as will adjusting the pressure on your pressure foot if possible.

LECTURE: ESTIMATING YARDAGE FOR A QUILT

How do you know how much fabric to purchase for a quilt? Walking into a quilt shop filled with hundreds of bolts of enticing fabrics can be an overwhelming experience, but having precise measurements in hand can help control the impulse to buy it all. Before you begin to figure the amount of fabric to buy, you need to have made basic decisions such as the pattern you will use, the placement of colors in the pattern, how you will set the blocks, and how wide any sashing or borders will be.

Let's assume you want to make a crib quilt using twelve 12" blocks and a 3" border all around. You decide to use the Churn Dash pattern and three fabrics; a print, a solid, and muslin.

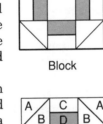

Block

There are three shapes in the pattern: a triangle (A and B), a rectangle (C and D), and a square (E). Each fabric has a different letter as label, even though the shape is the same.

Quilt Diagram

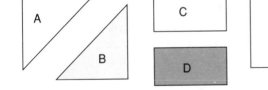

Pieces In Quilt

The chart on page 124 will help you determine how much of each fabric you will need.

STEP 1:

In the first column, enter the names of the shapes and the number of pieces to be cut from each fabric with that shape. For our Churn Dash crib quilt the chart would look like this:

    A....4 muslin
    B....4 print
    C....4 muslin
    D....4 solid
    E....l muslin

STEP 2:

At the top of Column 2, enter the number of blocks you need. Then multiply that number by the number of pieces of each entry in Column 1 and write that number in Column 2. For example, you will need 12 blocks for the Churn Dash crib quilt, so you need 48 pieces of A, 48 pieces of B, etc.

STEP 3:

Next, cut a piece of shelf paper or freezer paper 42" wide. This represents the width of a piece of fabric, minus the selvages. Using the templates for the pattern, mark a row across the paper as you would mark the fabric, keeping in mind the grain line and remembering to add seam allowances. For instance, piece E is a 4½" square, so you can get eight across the width of the fabric. Enter the number of pieces you can get in the width of the fabric for each shape in Column 3.

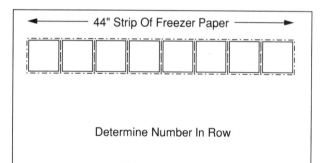

44" Strip Of Freezer Paper

Determine Number In Row

STEP 4:

Now measure the depth of the row of shapes you marked on the paper. For piece E, this is 4½". Enter this number in Column 4.

STEP 5:

The last step is calculation. Divide Column 3 into Column 2 for each shape. For piece E, divide 8 into 12. Since it doesn't divide evenly, use the next higher whole number, or 2. It will take 2 rows to cut all the E pieces you need. Multiply the result by Column 4. 2 x 4½" = 9". This is the length of fabric you will need in order to cut E. Enter this number in Column 5. Make the same computations in Column 5 for each shape.

STEP 6:

To find out how much you need of each fabric, use the second part of the chart marked Color. Enter the fabrics across the top, in this case, muslin, print, and solid. Under each color, list the amounts from Column 5.

STEP 7:

Figure the amount needed for the sashing and borders. If a 3" border is added to the quilt, the quilt will measure 36" + 6" by 48" + 6" for a finished size of 42" by 54". These measurements determine the length of the borders. Add ½" to each dimension for seam allowance, resulting in two pieces 3½" x 54½" and two pieces 3½" x 42½".

If at all possible, you should cut the borders in one piece, which means you would need a 55" length of fabric for the longest piece. If you cut all four border pieces side by side, you will only use 14" of the width of the fabric.

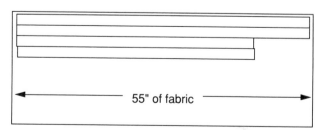

55" of fabric

If you will also be using the same fabric in the blocks, you will have enough to cut the pieces from what is left after the borders are cut. If you are not using the border fabric in the piecing, you will have fabric left over to use in another quilt.

If you would rather not have fabric left over, it is possible to cut the border pieces across the width of the fabric. The 42½" pieces will probably fit without piecing, but you will need to piece the longer 54" pieces. Be sure the seams are symmetrical and prints, if any, match. You would need 21" of fabric to cut the borders crosswise.

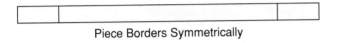

Piece Borders Symmetrically

Enter the amount of fabric you will need for borders, (and sashing if any) under the appropriate color column.

STEP 8 :

Binding for the edge of the quilt can be cut acoss the grain of the fabric and seamed into a long strip. It should be 2" wide and as long as the perimeter of the quilt. The crib quilt is 192" around, and would take 5 strips of 42" fabric. Since each strip is 2" wide, this will require a total of 10". Enter the binding figure in the appropriate color column.

STEP 9:

Since the finished quilt is 42" wide, you will need only one length of fabric (54") for the backing. If a quilt is 44" to 87" wide, it will take two lengths of fabric, and if it is over 87", you will need three lengths. Enter the amount for the backing in the appropriate color column.

STEP 10:

Add all the figures in each color column to find the number of inches you need of each fabric. Divide this number by 36 to find the number of yards. *Always add* 10% to 20% as a safeguard. Fabric may shrink or be flawed, or you may make a mistake. You can always use the leftovers in a scrap quilt.

CHART FOR ESTIMATING QUILT YARDAGE					
Column 1 Piece/No. & Color	Column 2 Times No. Of Blocks	Column 3 No. Of Pieces In 44"	Column 4 Depth Of Row	Column 5 $\dfrac{\text{Column 2}}{\text{Column 3}}$ Times Column 4	
Color					
Amount Required					
Total					
Add 10%-20%					

Home Study Course
in
Quiltmaking

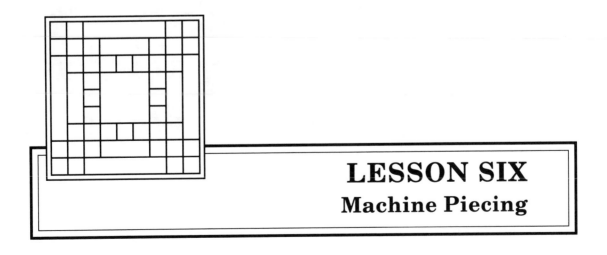

LESSON SIX
Machine Piecing

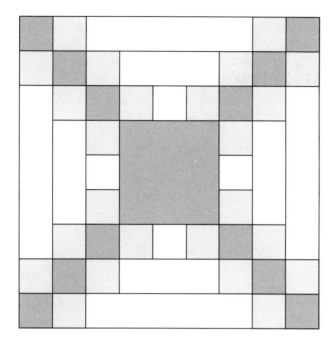

Pattern A: **Desperation**, *Beginner Level*

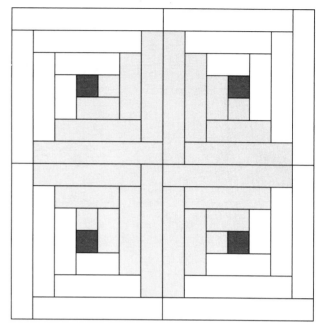

Pattern B: **Log Cabin**, *Intermediate Level*

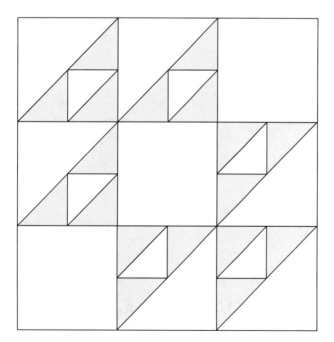

Pattern C: **Cat's Cradle**, *Intermediate Level*

Pattern D: **Seminole Star**, *Challenge Level*

LESSON SIX: MACHINE PIECING

To use this lesson, first read its Introduction and its General Instructions. If you are making the wallhanging, decide which pattern you would like to make. Each one has the difficulty level indicated so that you can take into account your own skills, interest, and time. If you are making the full-size quilt, you will want to complete all of the blocks.

> *Note: If you want to construct a top and use a frame to baste and quilt, see Lesson Ten: Section Two.*

INTRODUCTION TO MACHINE PIECING

As mentioned in the introduction to the previous lesson, quiltmakers were quick to use the newly-invented sewing machine to piece quilt tops. For a long time, though, it was considered not quite "proper," as if the quilter were trying to deceive others about the amount of work that went into a top. Only recently have competitions allowed machine and hand-pieced quilts to be judged in the same categories (which is practical, since the only way to tell the difference visually is to pull the seam apart). For the most part, blocks were constructed by machine in the same stitching sequence as they had been hand-done, saving stitching time, but not taking full advantage of the new technology.

At the same time as quilters were using the machine to piece tops, the Seminole Indians in Florida were using the machine to develop an unusual style of characteristic trim, which involved tearing strips of fabric, stitching them together, then re-cutting and stitching them again until very intricate-looking designs evolved. In the 1970s, several quilters, among them Barbara Johannah and Blanche and Helen Young, discovered that by using the principles of Seminole piecing, traditional quilt patterns could be constructed quickly and precisely, thereby opening up a whole new quiltmaking technology. See the illustration below. Rotary cutters and mats are very useful tools to increase precision in cutting, but careful marking with a ruler and cutting with scissors will work.

One drawback to the techniques which we will utilize in this lesson is the need to work at a table and a sewing machine, instead of relaxing in a favorite chair with handwork.

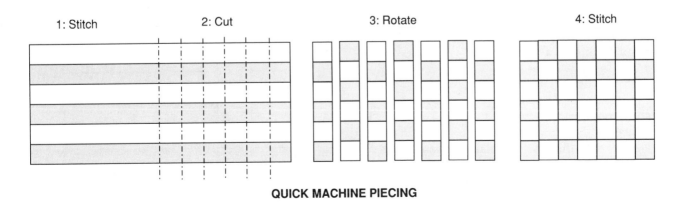

1: Stitch   2: Cut   3: Rotate   4: Stitch

QUICK MACHINE PIECING

GENERAL INSTRUCTIONS

Cutting Fabric

Where template patterns are given, they already include the ¼" seam allowance. Note these are different from templates for hand piecing, which do *not* include seam allowance since the stitching line is followed. When machine-piecing, it is more important to be able to match the cut edges accurately, so the template patterns *include* the seam allowance.

Cutting accurate strips of fabric is essential. It is easiest and most accurate to use a rotary cutter, cutting ruler, and mat, although careful marking with pencil and ruler and careful cutting with scissors will also work.

You can cut six to eight layers of fabric at a time with the rotary cutter. Fold the fabric in layers, place it on the mat, and use the cutting ruler as a straight-edge to guide the cutter. If your mat has a grid, you can also use it to line up the ruler.

Always sheath the cutter when you put it down, even for a moment! It is extremely sharp and dangerous.

Stitching

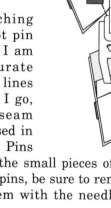

Thread color should blend with the fabrics being stitched. When stitching small pieces together, chain-piece all units of one operation before cutting the thread.

For most stitching operations, I do not pin the edges together. I am usually more accurate matching the seam lines with my fingers as I go, especially if the seam allowances are pressed in alternate directions. Pins also tend to distort the small pieces of fabric. If you do decide to use pins, be sure to remove them when you reach them with the needle. Do not stitch over them.

Pressing

Lay the stitched strips right side up on the ironing board and use the tip of your iron to open pieces. Be careful to keep the seam straight and not distort it. Seams must be pressed before cutting or stitching again. In general, you should always press seams in the same direction during any operation, unless otherwise instructed. This usually results in seams that lie in opposite directions when they meet, which adds to accuracy.

Checking Seam Width

It is necessary to check your seam allowance width before starting, because you will not mark a seam line on the fabric before piecing. Cut 5 strips of any fabric, each 1" wide and 6" long. Stitch the strips together with a ¼" seam using the guide on your machine (or the edge of the presser foot), with 12 - 15 stitches per inch.

Press, as described above.

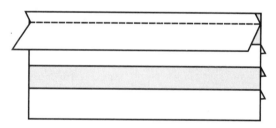

Measure the width of the center strips. Each should be exactly ½". If any are not, do the exercise again, adjusting the seam allowance width. Keep trying until you can stitch strips exactly ½" wide.

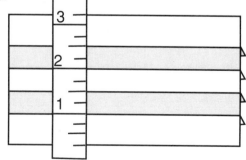

Mark your machine with tape at the correct position for edge of fabric.

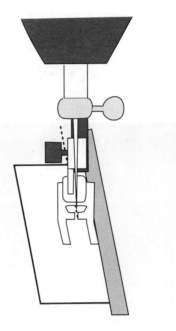

Examine the stitching to be sure the fabric is not puckered along the seam. If it is not perfectly flat, loosen the stitch tension very slightly or decrease the pressure on the presser foot until seams are smooth.

Quilting

These blocks provide a good opportunity to practice your machine quilting skills from the last lesson. Several of the patterns have so many seam allowances they would be difficult to hand quilt. Be sure to pin generously to prevent fabric slipping. In general, I think it is appropriate to hand quilt either hand-pieced or machine-pieced blocks, but I don't feel machine quilting is appropriate for hand-pieced blocks.

In any case, whenever you plan to quilt "in the ditch," that is, along the seam lines of the pieces in a block, you might as well do it by machine since the stitching will not be very visible.

Pattern A: **Desperation**, *Beginner Level*

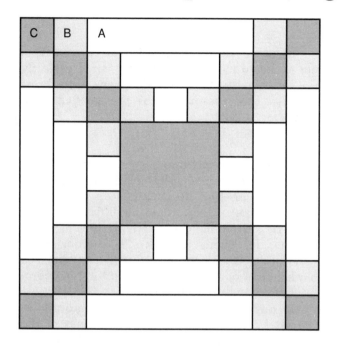

The pattern for this block comes from an old quilt top I purchased several years ago. The top dates from the late 1800s, and I call it a "desperation quilt," because it is obvious the maker went to great lengths to salvage enough fabric to make the design. She incorporated used muslin and pieced three or four scraps of fabric to make the 1" squares.

STEP 1:

Cut the fabric pieces.

Fabric A: Cut a piece 6½" wide and 11⅝" long. Cut three pieces from it: 1⅝", 3⅞", and 6⅛".

Fabric B: Cut a strip 1⅝" wide and 39" long. Cut four pieces from it, 6½" long.

Fabric C: Cut a strip 1⅝" wide and 19½" long. Cut four pieces from it, 3¼" long.

Make a template from the pattern on page 132 for the center square. Mark and cut one piece from Fabric C. (Remember, do not add seam allowance.)

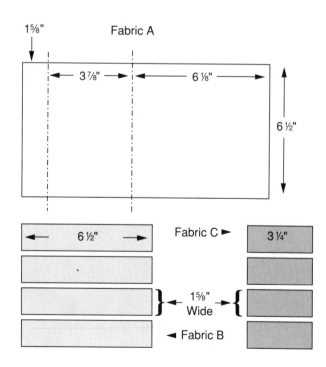

STEP 2:

Stitch strips together following diagram. Use ¼" seam allowance as determined in the General Instructions. Press all seams in the same direction.

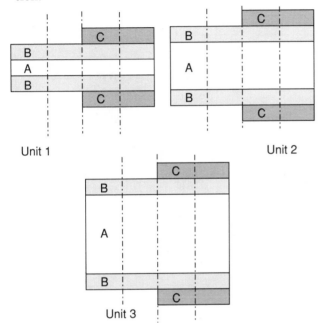

Unit 1   Unit 2

Unit 3

STEP 3:

Cut each unit from STEP 1 into strips 1⅝" wide. Lay out pieces as shown and pin to layout.

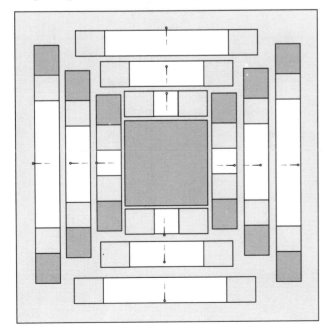

STEP 4:

Stitch strips in the following sequence:

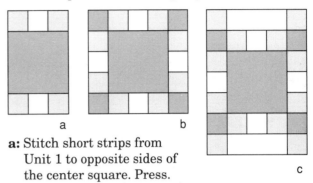

a   b

c

a: Stitch short strips from Unit 1 to opposite sides of the center square. Press.

b: Stitch long strips from Unit 1 to the remaining sides of the center square, matching seams. Press.

c: Stitch short strips from Unit 2 to the opposite sides of the center unit, matching seams. Press.

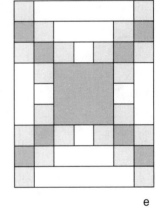

d

e

d: Stitch long strips from Unit 2 to the remaining sides of the center unit, matching seams. Press.

e: Stitch short strips from Unit 3 to opposite sides of the center unit, matching seams. Press.

f: Stitch long strips from Unit 3 to the remaining sides of the center unit, matching seams. Press.

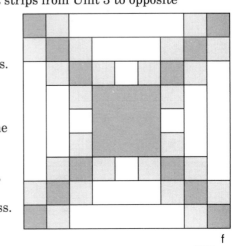

f

STEP 5:

Baste and pin for machine quilting.

Suggested quilting design

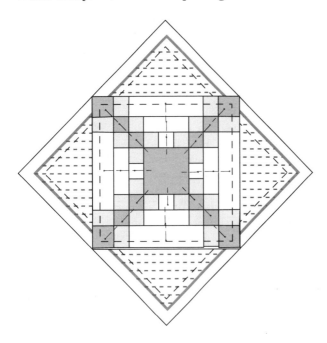

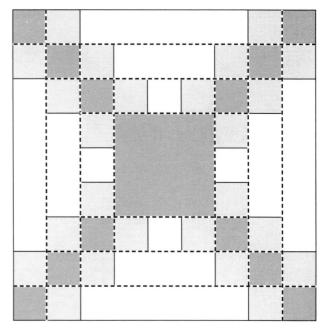

TEMPLATE PATTERN

Pattern B: **Log Cabin**, *Intermediate Level*

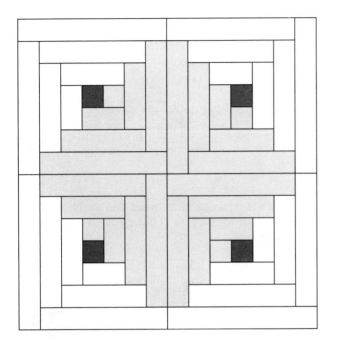

The Log Cabin is one of the oldest known pieced patterns. An Egyptian mummy was found wrapped in a fabric pieced in this way. The name we know the pattern by probably resulted from its construction being similar to that of log buildings in pioneer America. The term "Log Cabin" refers not only to the familiar pattern but also to a method of construction which can be used for a wide variety of patterns. In fact, the Desperation block utilized the same construction method.

Basically, construction begins at the center of the block. Strips are added around the sides, either symmetrically or spirally, until the edge of the block is reached. In American patchwork tradition, if the center square was red or yellow, it symbolized the hearth fire, the heart of the home. If the block was diagonally light and dark, it symbolized the joy and sorrow of everyday life.

STEP 1:

Cut fabric.

Fabric A: Make a template from the pattern
below and cut four center squares.

Fabric B (light):
Cut 1⅛" wide strips for the rows.
    Row 1, 15"
    Row 2, 25"
    Row 3, 34"

Fabric C (dark):
Cut 1⅛" wide strips
for the rows.
    Row 1, 20"
    Row 2, 30"
    Row 3, 38"

```
┌─────────────────────┐
│                     │
│                     │
│                     │
│   CENTER SQUARE     │
│   PATTERN           │
│                     │
│                     │
│                     │
└─────────────────────┘
```

STEP 2:

Stitch Row 1 in the following sequence:

a: Stitch four center squares to the Row 1 light
strip. Cut apart and press.

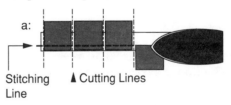

b: Rotate the pieces 90 degrees and stitch them to
the remainder of the Row 1 light strip. Cut
apart and press.

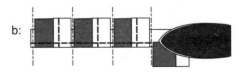

c: Rotate the pieces 90 degrees and stitch them to
the Row 1 dark strip. Cut apart and press.

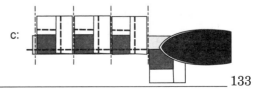

d: Rotate the pieces 90 degress and stitch them to the remainder of the Row 1 dark strip. Cut apart and press. This completes the first row around the center square.

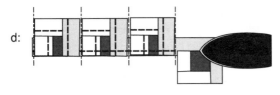

STEP 3:

Stitch Row 2.

a: Stitch the four squares to the Row 2 light strip. Cut apart and press.

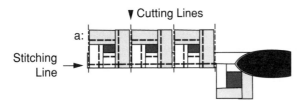

b: Rotate the pieces 90 degrees and stitch them to the remainder of the Row 2 light strip. Cut apart and press.

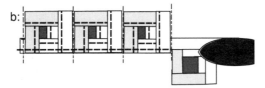

c: Rotate the pieces 90 degrees and stitch them to the Row 2 dark strip. Cut apart and press.

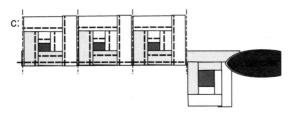

d) Rotate the pieces 90 degress and stitch them to the remainder of the Row 2 dark strip. Cut apart and press. This completes the second row around the center square.

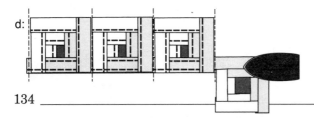

STEP 4:

Stitch Row 3.

a: Stitch the four squares to Row 3 light strip. Cut apart and press.

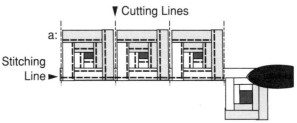

b: Rotate the pieces 90 degrees and stitch to the remainder of the Row 3 light strip. Cut apart and press.

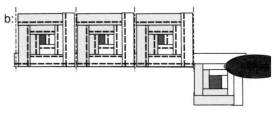

c: Rotate the pieces 90 degrees and stitch to the Row 3 dark strip. Cut apart and press.

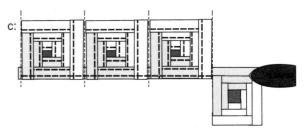

d: Rotate the pieces 90 degress and stitch to the remainder of the Row 3 dark strip. Cut apart and press. This completes the last row around the center square.

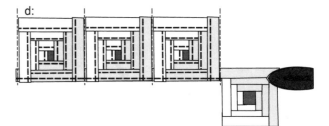

STEP 5:

Arrange the four blocks as you wish; then stitch them together, using a ¼" seam allowance. Some possible arrangements are illustrated below.

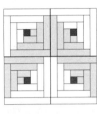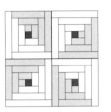

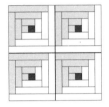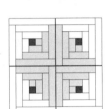

STEP 6:

Baste and pin for quilting.

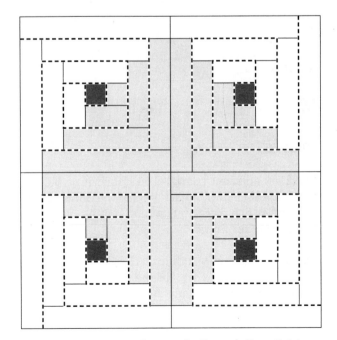

Suggested quilting design: Quilt each Log Cabin in a spiral in the ditch, beginning with the last "log" added to the block and ending around the center square.

Pattern C: **Cat's Cradle**, *Intermediate Level*

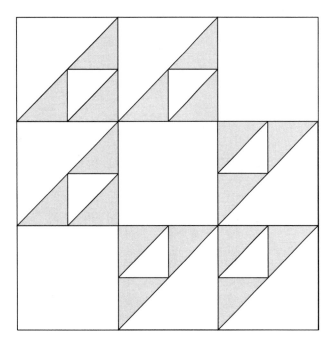

The name of this pattern comes from a string figure in a children's game.

STEP 1:

Prepare templates from the patterns on page 139.

STEP 2:

Mark six adjacent triangles on Fabric A or B. Mark another line ¼" each side of the diagonal. Cut out as one piece and cut a matching piece from the other fabric.

Stitch both layers together on the ¼" lines. Cut the squares apart; then cut the triangles apart on the diagonal. Press seams toward the dark fabric.

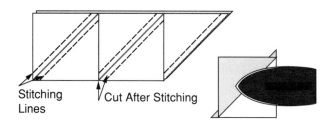

Stitching Lines

Cut After Stitching

STEP 3:

Cut a strip from Fabric B, 3" x 16".

Stitch the squares from STEP 2 to the strip as indicated on the diagram. Press seams toward the dark fabric, and then cut apart as indicated, cutting the vertical lines first, then the angles.

STEP 4:

Stitch the units from STEP 2 to the remainder of Fabric B. Do not overlap seam allowances. Press the seam toward the dark fabric, and then cut as indicated. Be sure to cut from the seam allowance to the seam allowance.

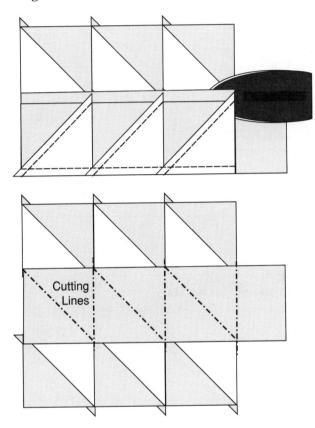

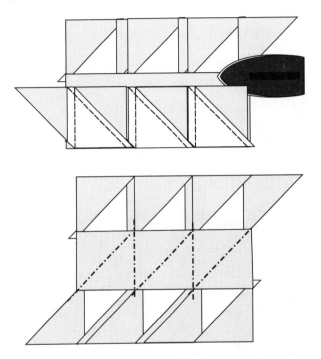

STEP 5:

Cut a strip of Fabric A, 4¾" x 13½". Lay the completed triangles right side down on the strip, forming squares as shown. Stitch on the diagonal seam lines; then cut the triangles apart, and press seams to the dark fabric.

Pin the completed squares to the layout backing in the correct position.

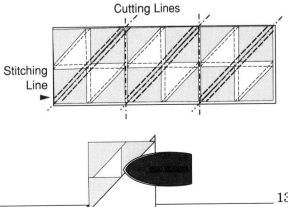

STEP 6:

Using a square template made from the pattern on the next page, cut three squares from Fabric B. Pin to the layout backing.

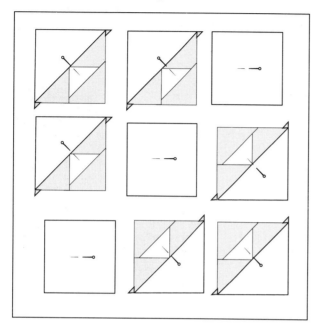

b: Stitch the rows together. Press.

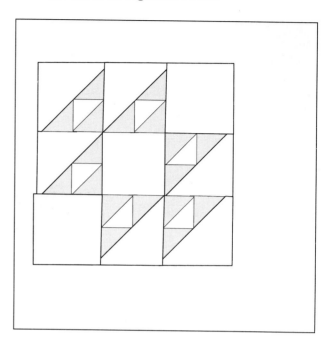

STEP 7:

a: Stitch the squares in each row together, pressing seams in alternate directions.

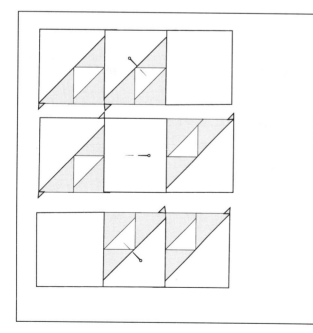

STEP 8:
Baste and pin for quilting.

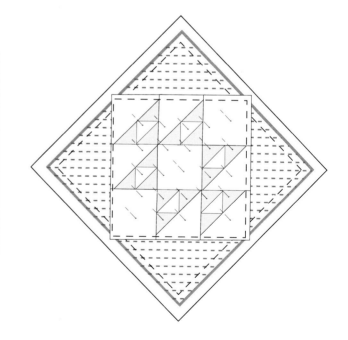

I have machine quilted this block in a continuous curve design, a concept developed by Barbara Johannah of California. The slight curve softens the pattern of the block in much the same way that the traditional quilting inside the seam line does. The diagram shows the stitching sequence I used.

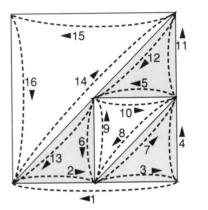

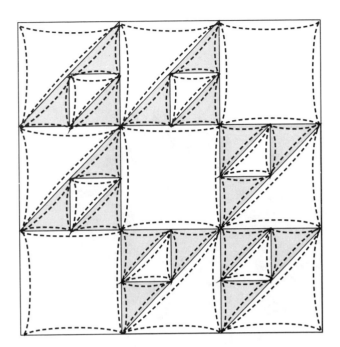

Suggested quilting design

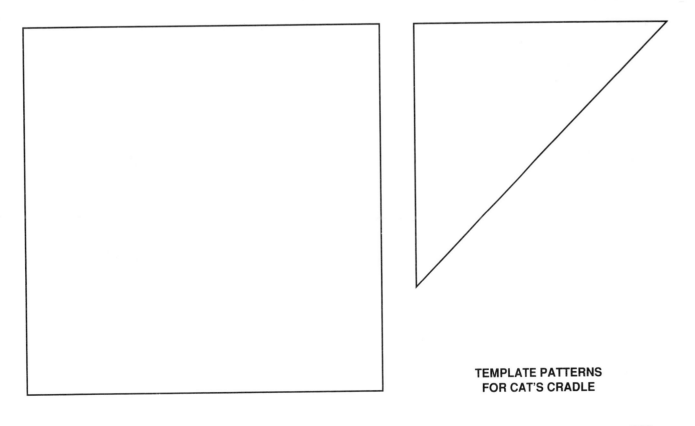

**TEMPLATE PATTERNS
FOR CAT'S CRADLE**

Pattern D: **Seminole Star**, *Challenge Level*

This design which seems very intricate is made utilizing the strip piecing technique developed by the Seminole Indians. Be sure to work carefully and accurately.

STEP 1:

Cut fabric strips 1⅛" x 30" as follows:
Fabric A: 1   Fabric B: 2
Fabric C: 3   Fabric D: 2

Arrange the strips right side up according to the diagram below.

STEP 2:

a: Turn Fabric D right side down over Fabric C. Repeat with B over A, C over D, and C over B. Stitch the pairs together, always stitching the top edge. Press all the seams toward the bottom fabric.

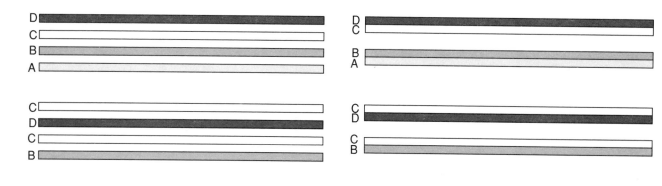

b: Arrange the strips right side up in the same order as STEP 2. Pick up the D/C strip and turn it right side down over the B/A strip. Repeat with the C/D strip over the C/B strip. Stitch pairs together on the top edge. Press the seams in the same direction.

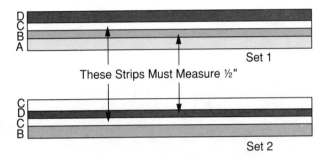

Hint: Use your fingers to line up the stitched seam allowances. Check to make sure the fabrics in each strip are in the same order they were in STEP 2. Make sure stitched strips measure ½" in width.

STEP 3:

Make a template from the cutting guide pattern. Place Set 1 of the stitched strips right side down on a cutting surface with the fabrics in the same order. Place Set 2 over it, right side down, matching seam allowances and edges. Use the template to mark off 16 pieces. Mark a ¼" seam line on each side of the template line. Cut both layers on the template line.

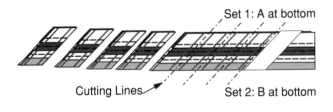

STEP 4:

Place a Set 2 piece over a Set 1 piece, right sides together, and stitch as indicated. Be sure the seams cross at the seam line. Repeat for the remaining pieces. Press seams.

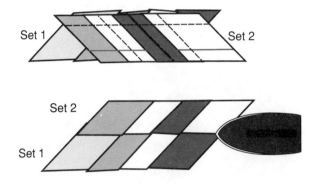

STEP 5:

Place two pieces from STEP 4 right sides together, and stitch.

Tip: The A fabrics should be visible at each end.

Repeat for remaining pieces, forming 8 diamonds.

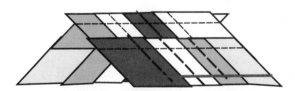

STEP 6:

Mark dots at the intersection of the seam lines on the diamonds as indicated. Stitch two diamonds together, from the outside dot to the center, matching seams, following the diagram below. Open and press seams in the same direction.

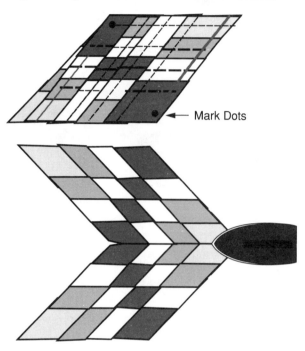

← Mark Dots

STEP 8:

Stitch halves together from dot to dot to form star. Match the intersection of the Y-seams. Open and press seam.

STEP 7:

Stitch pairs of diamonds together from dot to center, matching seams. Open and press seams in same direction as in STEP 6.

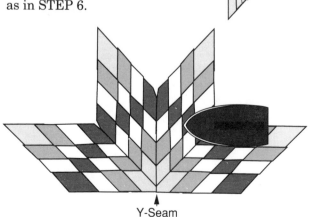

Y-Seam

STEP 9:

Make templates for the set-in square and triangle from the pattern. These are machine piecing templates, so do not add a seam allowance. Cut a small slit in the template so you can mark the position of the dot on the fabric. (If you have a ⅛" paper punch, you can punch a hole at the position of the dot.)

Mark and cut the fabric. It may be layered but be sure to mark the position of the dot on each piece. The grain line of the triangle should be parallel to the longest edge.

a: Pin the squares and triangles to one side of each star point, right sides together, alternating shapes. Pin through the dot of the square or triangle, and the dot of the diamond. The edge of the square will be at the point of the diamond, but the edge of the triangle will extend beyond it. Stitch the seam from the edge to the pin and backstitch to secure. Press the seam toward the square or triangle.

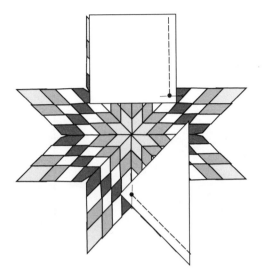

b: Swing the second seam allowance of the square or triangle to the opposite diamond, folding the first diamond out of the way so the seam will be flat for sewing. Pin through the dot of the square or triangle and the dot of the diamond. Stitch the seam. Press toward the square or triangle. Continue adding squares and triangles until the block is complete. Press the block.

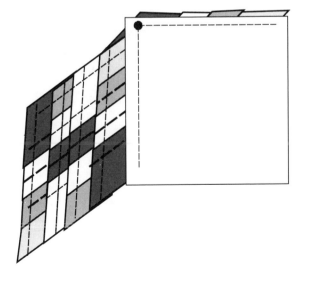

STEP 10:

Baste and pin for quilting.

The suggested quilting design is ⅛" inside the edges of set-in squares and triangles and in the ditch of the large diamonds.

Suggested quilting design

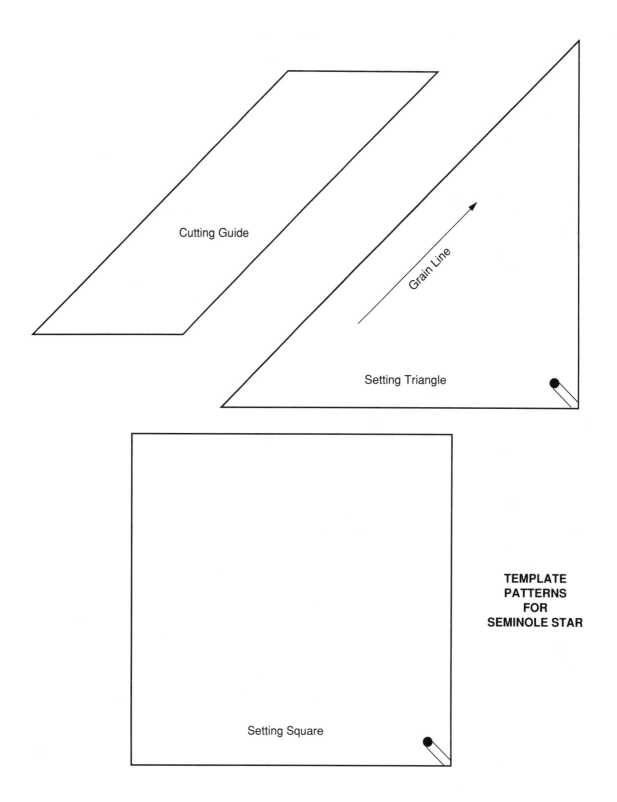

Cutting Guide

Grain Line

Setting Triangle

**TEMPLATE
PATTERNS
FOR
SEMINOLE STAR**

Setting Square

HOW ARE YOU DOING?

When you have finished your blocks, check them to see how well you are doing.

Piecing Technique:
• Strips should be even in width, and squares should be square. If they waver, one reason may be difficulty in maintaining a consistent seam allowance. Placing a strip of tape on the machine where the edge of the fabric should be will help.

• Seams should meet precisely at corners. Careful pressing, alternating the seams in opposite directions, and holding the seams together with your fingers for stitching will help.

General Appearance:
• Finished blocks should be square and not distorted. Careful measuring and cutting and consistent seam allowances are necessary. Also, use care when stitching over bulky seam allowances, so that the fabric is not distorted.

LECTURE: A SHORT HISTORY OF QUILTMAKING

Even before fabric was invented, people were sewing together pieces of skin to make larger pieces for clothing and covering. When fabric became available, it didn't take long before the pieces became regular and patterned. Fragments of patchwork and other evidence exist from many ancient civilizations, including Egypt, China, India, and Ancient Greece.

The idea of stitching three layers together for warmth and protection appears to have been brought to Europeans by returning Crusaders, who discovered their opponents wearing garments made this way to cushion their armor. The stitching, too, soon turned to a decorative element, as evidenced by the oldest fragments of quilting in existence. They were made in the 14th Century, and were hangings illustrating the story of Tristan and Isolde, using fine stitching and stuffed work. Quilting was often used for clothing as well.

A long period of very harsh winters in Europe led people to create bed quilts from two layers of fabric, stuffed with whatever was available for warmth, and stitched to hold the stuffing in place. These evolved into the beautifully designed and stitched whole-cloth quilts of more recent European history, some of which still survive.

Making quilts from block patterns apparently developed in the United States. In early America, settlers used every scrap of fabric available for clothing and bedcoverings, since it was either made at home or imported at a dear cost. It is easy to imagine patching upon patching to extend the life of well-used coverings, and cutting up useable parts of old clothes to make additional quilts. It is also easy to imagine that women found it necessary to create a little beauty in their lives by patterning the pieces into repetitive blocks and arranging the colors and fabrics in the scrap bag.

As life became easier and leisure time for needlework was available, as well as money to buy imported fabric, well-to-do women turned to applique (which is somewhat wasteful of fabric) to make "fancy" quilt tops. They showed off their needlework skills in the exquisite quilting as well. Some women made white-work quilts, whose only design came from the stitching. These quilts were family heirlooms, and many still survive today.

It is difficult for us today to realize how important quilting was in women's lives 150-200 years ago. All girls were expected to learn to sew, and making quilts was one of the household duties until the Industrial Revolution, when factory-made blankets could be bought. At that point, women apparently relished the freedom from such chores, and quiltmaking declined, except for the Crazy quilts of the Victorian era. Today we would call them a fad, but they were wonderful opportunities to show off.

After the first World War and during the Great Depression of the 1930s, there was a short revival of interest in quilting, perhaps fueled by the lack of income for more costly entertainment. Many scrap quilts, in patterns such as the Grandmother's Flower Garden, Dresden Plate, and Double Wedding Ring, still survive today. Magazines and newspapers regularly published patterns, and nationwide competitions were held. However, with the advent of World War II, women were needed in the work force to support the war effort, and quiltmaking died out again.

The most recent revival has come as a result of two factors: the first was an exhibit in 1971 by Jonathan Holstein and Gail van der Hoof at the Whitney Museum of American Art that presented quilts as art, and the second was the Bicentennial in 1976, which revived an interest in many early crafts, among them quilting. Since then, the world of quilters has been growing steadily, resulting in competitions, conferences, and exhibits all over the world. Many quilt magazines are now being published to satisfy quilters' appetite for inspiration and information.

It has been speculated that one of the reasons for quilting's popularity in the early years of our country's existence was the fact that it afforded women the opportunity to express themselves in a way that did not threaten the male-dominated world of art. Whether or not this is true, many of today's artists have turned to quiltmaking as a medium that is not only a link with previous history and tradition, but is also uniquely suited to expressing a woman's artistic statements. No one knows what the future holds, but as long as new quilters continue to discover the satisfaction of quiltmaking, the art and the craft will survive.

RESOURCE

Quilts in America, Patsy and Myron Orlofsky, McGraw Hill, 1974.

Home Study Course
in
Quiltmaking

LESSON SEVEN
Ethnic Applique

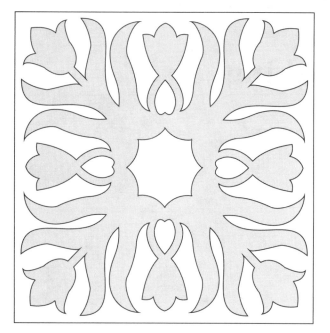

Pattern A: **Tulip Garden** (Hawaiian Applique)
Beginner Level

Pattern B: **Maze of Hearts** (Pa Ndau)
Intermediate Level

Pattern C: **Chintz Applique**, *Advanced Level*

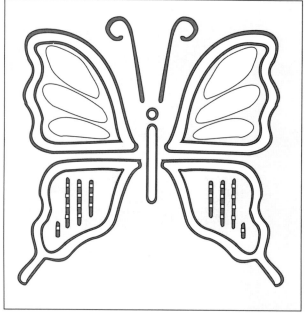

Pattern D: **Mola Butterfly**, *Challenge Level*

LESSON SEVEN: ETHNIC APPLIQUE

To use this lesson, first read its Introduction and its General Instructions. If you are making the wallhanging, decide which pattern you would like to make. Each one has the difficulty level indicated so that you can take into account your own skills, interest, and time. If you are making the full-size quilt, you will want to complete all of the blocks.

Note: If you want to construct a top and use a frame to baste and quilt, see Lesson Ten: Section Two.

INTRODUCTION TO ETHNIC APPLIQUE

Several widely separated cultures have independently developed unique styles of applique, which are used for a variety of cultural purposes. In this lesson, we will look at styles developed in the Hawaiian Islands; by the Hmong people in Laos, Cambodia, and Vietnam; by the Kuna Indians in the San Blas Islands of Central America; and also at a type of applique that was popular in the middle 1800s in the United States, which used printed fabric.

Hawaiian Applique

The wives of missionaries to the Hawaiian Islands brought their interest in quiltmaking along with them and taught the native women the needlework skills. The natives, however, did not see much point in cutting up whole pieces of fabric into little shapes and sewing them back together. They found that they could fold large pieces of fabric, cut the layers in designs that reflected the world around them, and applique the resulting shape to a large background piece of fabric. They drew inspiration from the abundance of flowers and other vegetation, and each quilter made a unique pattern which was not to be copied by others. The designs were "echo" quilted in expanding lines which followed the shapes of the pattern, similar to waves along the shore.

A full-size Hawaiian quilt is not a project to undertake lightly. It requires patience, skill, and a considerable amount of time, to accomplish.

Pa Ndau

The recent migration of many Hmong refugees from Cambodia has enriched the needlework vocabulary of quilters with "pa ndau" or "flower cloth." The Hmong tribes were farmers in the mountains, unschooled and living off the land, but of great value to American forces during the Vietnam conflict. After the fall of Saigon, the Communists took over Cambodia and began a systematic extermination of the Hmong people, many of whom fled to refugee camps in Thailand, and then to the United States.

Before the war, young girls were started on needlework as early as the age of three, and the skill they attained determined their marriageability. Each kin group developed a characteristic style of needlework which was used to embellish clothing, including cross-stitch, batik, and applique. However, it is the reverse-applique geometric designs of pa ndau that have attracted the attention and admiration of quilters.

Chintz Applique

The history of printed fabric is a fascinating one, involving tales of exploration and discovery as well as political power and intrigue. In the early years of the settlement of the United States, printed fabrics were very precious and difficult to obtain. In order to make them go farther, needleworkers cut floral prints apart and rearranged and appliqued them on a background fabric large enough for a quilt top. Eventually, during the 1800s, fabrics were even printed for just that purpose, and a piece might include a center basket of flowers, sprays or arrangements for smaller blocks, and rows of flowers for borders.

Molas

The Cuna Indians of the San Blas Islands in the Carribean used reverse applique on several layers of fabric to adorn panels which were used as the front and back of women's blouses. In contrast to the geometry of pa ndau, however, molas featured naturalistic designs of birds, animals, flowers, and even boats and airplanes.

RESOURCES

Creating Pa Ndau Applique, Carla J. Hassel, Wallace-Homestead Book Co., Lombard, IL, 1984.
Chintz Quilts, Unfading Glory, Lacy Folmar Bullard & Betty Jo Shiell, Serendipity Publishers, Tallahassee, FL, 1983.
Mola Making, Charlotte Patera, New Century Publishers, Piscataway, NJ, 1984.

GENERAL INSTRUCTIONS

Preparing a Background Block

Mark the seam line on a background block using the 10" square template. Follow the instructions for each pattern for marking, cutting and placing the appliques.

Stitching

All of the styles of applique in this lesson use the needle-turn method of hiding the raw edges described in Lesson Four, Pattern D: Grape Vine.

Hints:

Use your thumbnail to hold tiny curves in place for stitching.

Clip inside curves closely and shallowly where indicated.

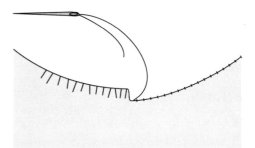

On sharp points, stitch up one side to the point, add an extra stitch to hold the point, and then turn under the allowance with the needle. Make small and close stitches to secure it.

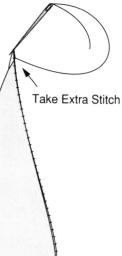

Take Extra Stitch

Pattern A: **Tulip Garden** (Hawaiian Applique), *Beginner Level*

The appliqued design in this technique is cut from a fabric square which has been folded in eighths, much like cutting paper snowflakes. The cut fabric is then carefully unfolded on the background block, basted, and appliqued.

STEP 1:

Trace the pattern on page 153 and cut it out of paper.

STEP 2:

Mark and cut a 10" square from fabric to be used for the applique design, using the background block template. Fold in eighths as shown, pressing each crease as sharp as possible. Fold the final triangles in opposite directions.

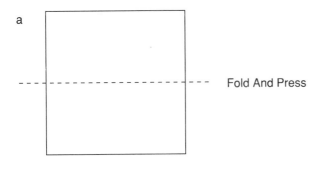

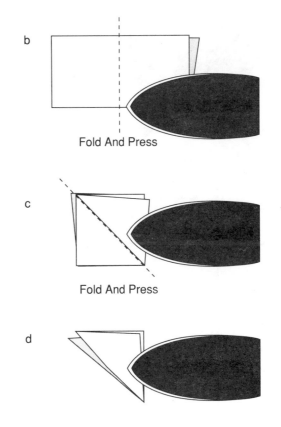

STEP 3:

Baste the whole surface of the folded piece.

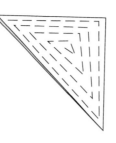

STEP 4:

Mark around the paper pattern on the folded and basted fabric.

STEP 5:

Carefully cut on the marked lines, through the basting threads. Remove the basting, but *do not* unfold yet.

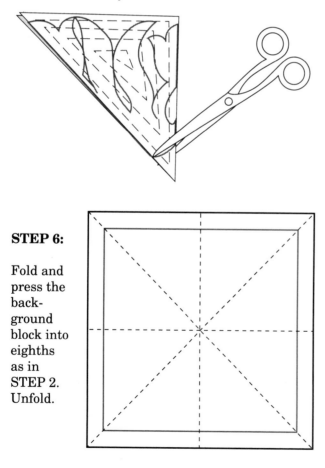

STEP 6:

Fold and press the background block into eighths as in STEP 2. Unfold.

STEP 7:

Working flat on a table, lay the cutout fabric on the background block, matching the folds. Unfold very carefully, keeping fabric as flat as possible. (It may be helpful to press the two fabrics together before basting.) Baste around the entire edge of the cut fabric, about ¼" in from the raw edges.

STEP 8:

Stitch the center first. Use short lengths of matching thread. Begin by using the needle to turn under a tiny seam allowance for about ½" in the center of one of the curves. (Amount to turn under will vary with the fabric. It should be just enough to secure the raw edges, ¹⁄₁₆" or less.) Hold it with your thumbnail and bring the needle up from underneath the block to just catch a thread of the fold. Make one stitch over the edge in place, then use a small traditional applique stitch (Lesson Four) to stitch the turned area. Use the nee-

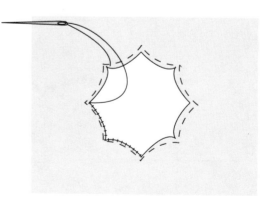

dle to turn under small amounts ahead of the stitching. Do not clip any points or curves. Use tighter stitches at the inside points.

Stitch inside hearts, using the same technique.

Stitch the outside edges. Work carefully to keep curves smooth and symmetrical.

Quilt outside the edges of the applique. Traditional Hawaiian Quilting would add concentric lines inside and outside the applique.

Suggested quilting design

STEP 9:

Baste the completed block to the backing and batting.

TULIP GARDEN PATTERN

Pattern B: **Maze of Hearts** (Pa Ndau), *Intermediate Level*

Part of the reverse applique pattern is cut into the top layer of fabric, much like the Hawaiian applique method, before it is basted to the background layer. After it has been stitched, the outline design is cut and stitched a little at a time. Try to make the channels an even ¼", and the same width as the remaining fabric in the spirals.

STEP 1:

Trace pattern on page 157 on paper and cut it out.

STEP 2:

Mark a 10" square on the fabric to be used for the applique; then add ½" seam allowances before cutting. Fold top fabric in eigths as shown, pressing creases. Fold the final triangles in opposite directions. Baste the whole surface of the folded piece.

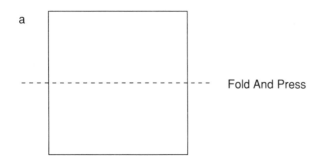

a

Fold And Press

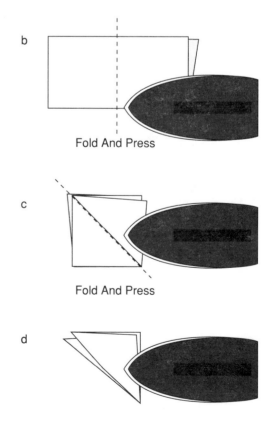

b

Fold And Press

c

Fold And Press

d

STEP 3:

Baste the paper pattern on the fabric.

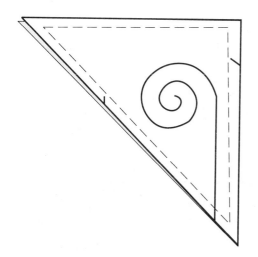

STEP 4:

Cut the spiral and the slits indicated. Carefully remove the basting and the pattern, but *do not* unfold yet.

STEP 5:

Fold the background square into eighths and press creases.

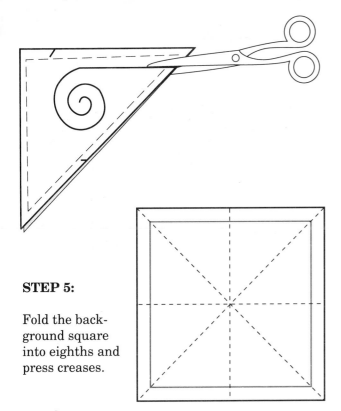

STEP 6:

Working flat on a table, unfold the background square; then lay the cut fabric over it, matching creases. Unfold the cut fabric *very* carefully, and lay the spirals flat, raw edges meeting. Baste ¼" on either side of the cut lines and 1" outside the spirals.

STEP 7:

a: Begin stitching on the convex curve at the center of a spiral. Depending on which is the most comfortable way to stitch, it can be either the right or left spiral. Remove basting when it's in the way. With the needle, turn under a tiny seam allowance for about ½", adjusting it with the needle so the curve is smooth. Bring the needle up from the back of the background block, catching a thread of the fold. Take an extra stitch to secure the thread, then continue around the curve with very small traditional applique stitches, as described in Lesson Four.

b: When you reach the point of the heart, secure the corner with an extra stitch before tucking under the adjacent edge with the needle. When you reach the center of the spiral on the opposite side of the heart, twirl the needle in the edge to make a smoothly rounded channel end. Secure with very tiny stitches.

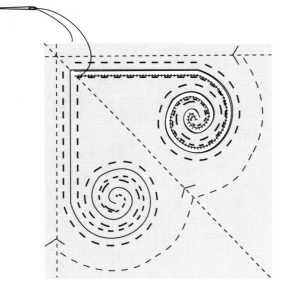

c: Begin stitching the concave curve back to the opposite side. Before turning under the edge with your needle, clip very closely with short snips, for a distance of about ½" at a time. Try to keep the channel an even width, and the same width as the spiral. When you reach the point of the heart, make a diagonal clip at the corner, the width of the seam allowance you are turning under. Continue to the center of the spiral where you began stitching. Round the end of the channel as in STEP 7b. Stitch the remaining hearts in the same way.

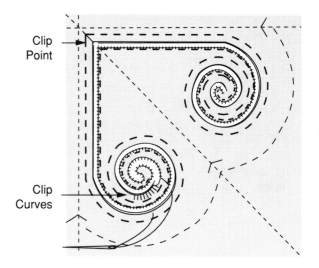

Clip Point

Clip Curves

STEP 8:

Beginning at one of the slits, cut about 1" of a line parallel to the outside of the heart spirals. (If you would be more comfortable with a marked line,

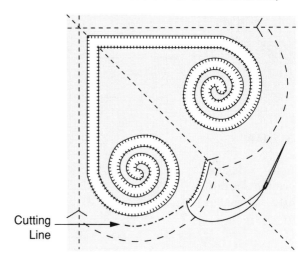

Cutting Line

draw it around the spirals, parallel to them and at a distance equal to the clips.) Stitch the convex side of the cut line. Continue to cut and stitch until you reach the end of a thread; then go back and catch up with the concave curve.

STEP 9:

Baste to backing and batting.

Quilt around the heart shapes.

Suggested quilting design

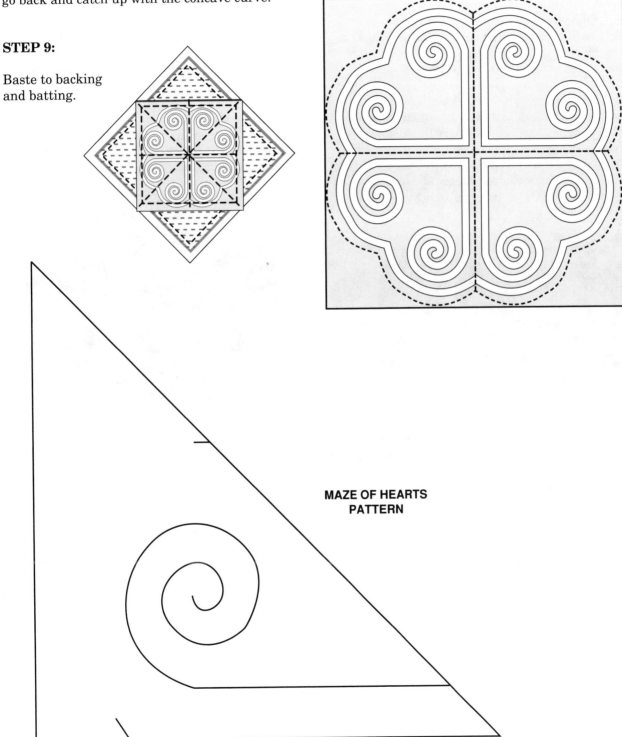

**MAZE OF HEARTS
PATTERN**

Pattern C: **Chintz Applique**, *Advanced Level*

You will need a small amount of additional fabric for this block. Fabric for chintz applique should be firmly woven but not too heavy or it will be difficult to turn the edges under. Look for motifs 2" to 3" in diameter that can be cut out and arranged in a pleasing pattern. I was able to find a 100% cotton quilt fabric with the right colors, but you may need to look at dress fabrics or in the decorating fabric section for curtain fabrics. It is nice but not necessary for the fabric to have a sheen. You are not limited to flowers but may use any printed motif you like that will fit in the space. For instance, you could use toys or animals for a child, or birds or scenic motifs. Use your imagination.

Ideas for chintz applique.

STEP 1:

Roughly cut a number of motifs from the chintz fabric. Be sure to leave at least ⅛" seam allowance around the area you plan to applique. Play with the pieces on your background block, arranging them in several different ways until you find one you like. I made a wreath with mine, partly because they were all identical, but you might like a bouquet instead. If you choose a large motif, you may be able to fit only one of them on the block, and then cut smaller pieces to add to it.

Arrange cutout motifs.

STEP 2:

When you have an arrangement you like, pin the pieces to the background. (Safety pins will hold them firmly until you get to them.)

STEP 3:

If pieces overlap, you will need to start with the bottom one. Pin the edges of the pieces on top of it out of the way to stitch. Use the needle to turn under the edge so that as little as possible of the shape is lost. You most likely will not be able to include all the points and curves when you stitch. Note the edges of the leaves in the photograph.

When you come to inside points, use very small stitches to prevent ravelling of the seam allowance. Continue to stitch down the motifs, working from the bottom layer to the top.

STEP 4:

Antique quilts with this kind of applique often had elaborate quilting as well, with blank spaces filled with feathers and flowers, and a diamond grid as a background. Chose a quilting pattern you feel will complement your design.

Baste the completed block to the backing and batting after marking the pattern.

Detail of applique stitching.

Pattern D: **Mola Butterfly**, *Challenge Level*

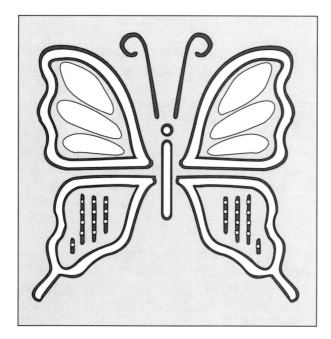

Two layers of 11" square fabrics are reverse appliqued to a background block in this pattern. The middle layer shows just as an outline. In addition, decorative shapes are added to the wings as a fourth layer.

STEP 1:

Mark a 10" square on two fabrics for the middle and top applique layers. Add ½" seam allowances and cut out.

STEP 2:

Trace Pattern A on pages 164 and 165. Mark the pattern on the middle layer of fabric.

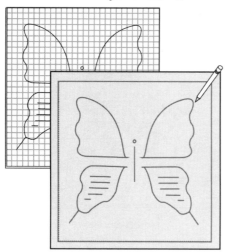

Baste the marked fabric to the background block around the edges of the pattern.

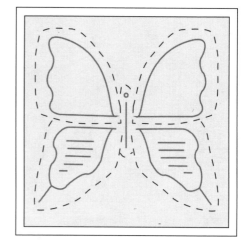

STEP 3:

a: Begin stitching with the body. Carefully cut *only* the middle layer on the pattern line for about 1". (Use a pin to pull the layers of fabric apart to start the cut.) Turn under a very tiny seam allowance along the cut edge. Bring the needle up through the background block through the very edge of the fold, catching a couple threads. Take another stitch to secure the start; then stitch about ½", using a small traditional applique stitch.

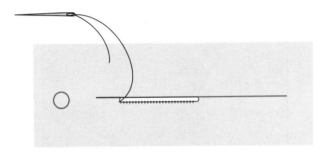

b: Cut another ½", then stitch, and repeat until you come to the end of the line. Twirl the needle in the end of the channel to get a smooth curve, and stitch with tiny stitches. Continue back along the body, keeping the channel an even ¼". Use the needle to make a smooth curve in the other end of the channel; then continue stitching to the start.

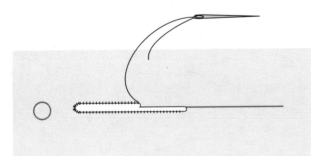

c: To stitch the dot for the head, cut as shown. Twirl the needle in the opening to round the shape as much as possible, and stitch with tiny stitches.

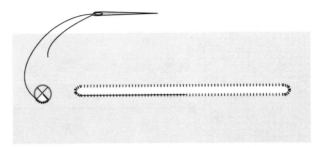

d: Cut and stitch a channel around the wings in the same fashion.

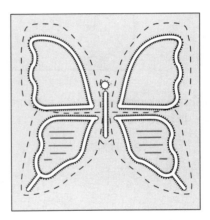

e: Cut slits in the lower wings one at a time and stitch the edges. Remove the basting.

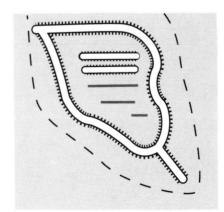

STEP 4:

a: Trace the lines for the antennae and slits from Pattern B (pages 166-167) on the top applique layer. Baste the top layer to the first two around the edges.

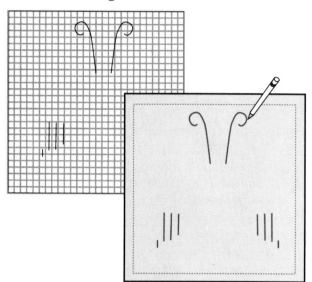

b: Turn the block over and baste around the stitched shapes from the back.

Back Of Block

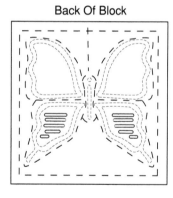

c: Turn the block right side up and lay it flat on a table. Using your fingernail, mark the edges of the channels that were stitched in the middle layer. (If you are using a print fabric for the top layer or can't see your mark, use a light box or tape the block to a window and trace the edges with a marking pencil.)

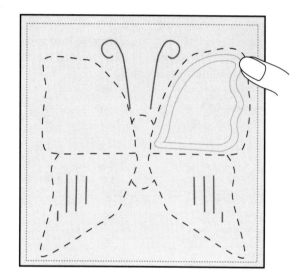

STEP 5:

a: Carefully cut a slit in the marked line on the edge of the body for about 1". Turn the inside edge in about ⅛" (so that ⅛" of the middle layer shows) and stitch. Try to keep the middle layer outline even. Continue to cut and stitch around the body. (You will be cutting away a small strip of fabric the size of the channel.)

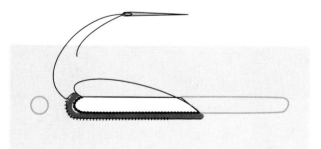

b: Repeat the cutting and stitching for the other shapes.

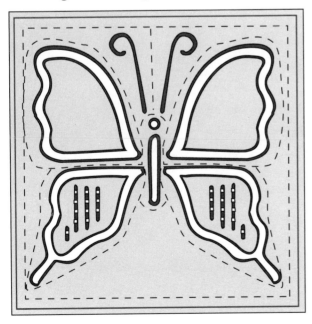

c: Cut and stitch the antennae according to STEP 3, a and b.

Using a light box, or holding the block to the light, make sure the vertical slits marked on the lower wings cross the horizontal slits in the middle layer. If not, redraw the slits before cutting and stitching.

STEP 6:

Cut out the additional fabric shapes for the upper wings from Pattern B, adding ⅛" seam allowances. Applique them in place.

STEP 7:

This block has too many layers to quilt. Baste it around the edges, to the backing and batting.

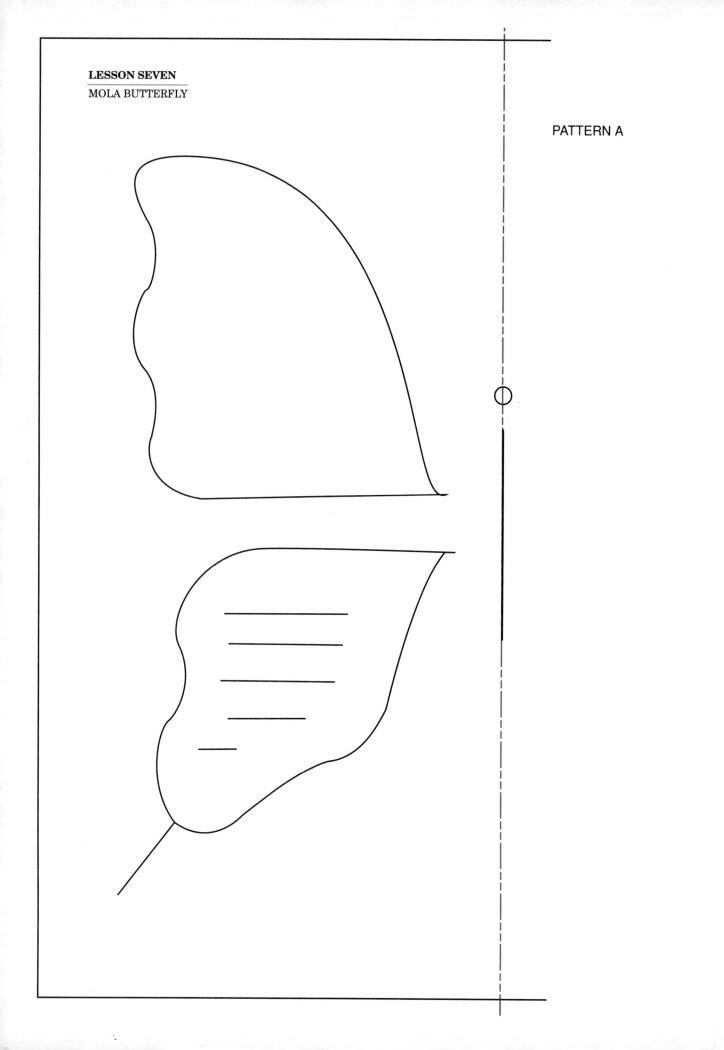

PATTERN A

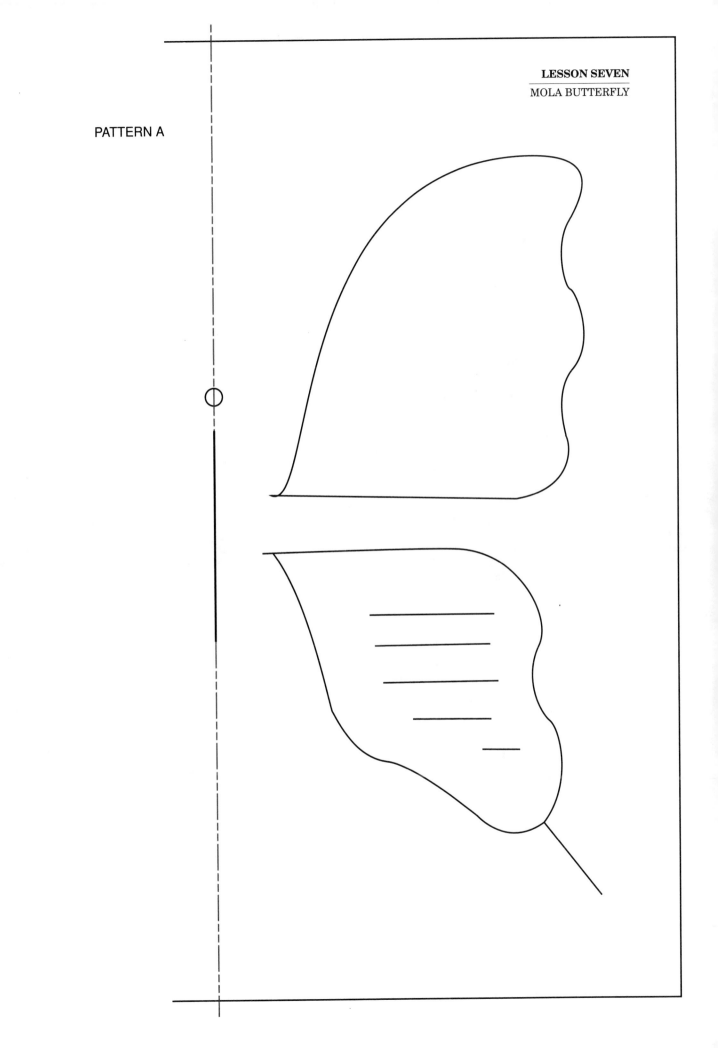

PATTERN A

PATTERN B

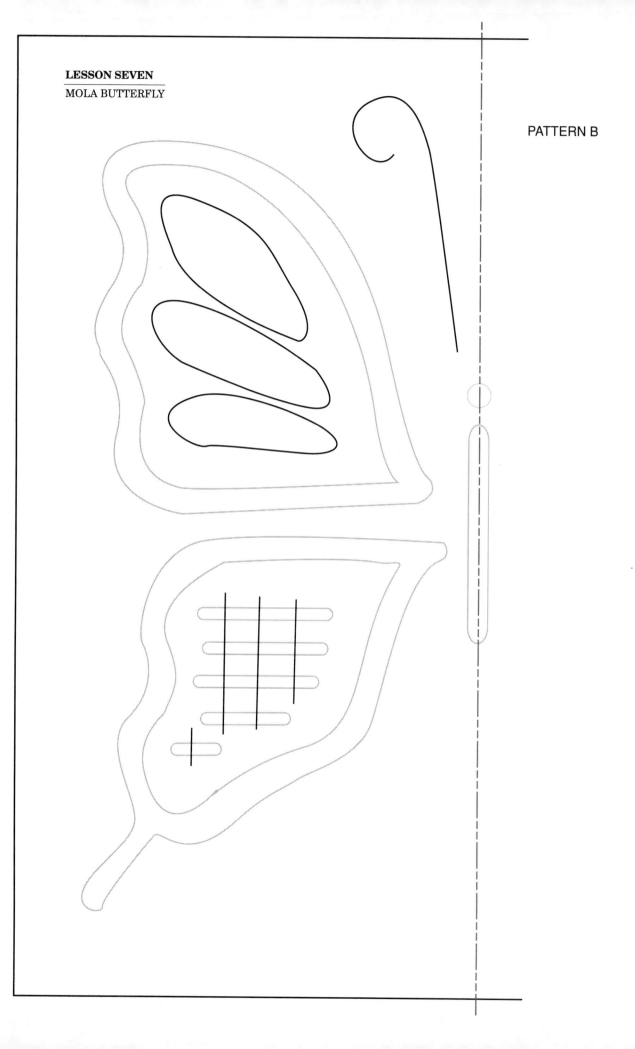

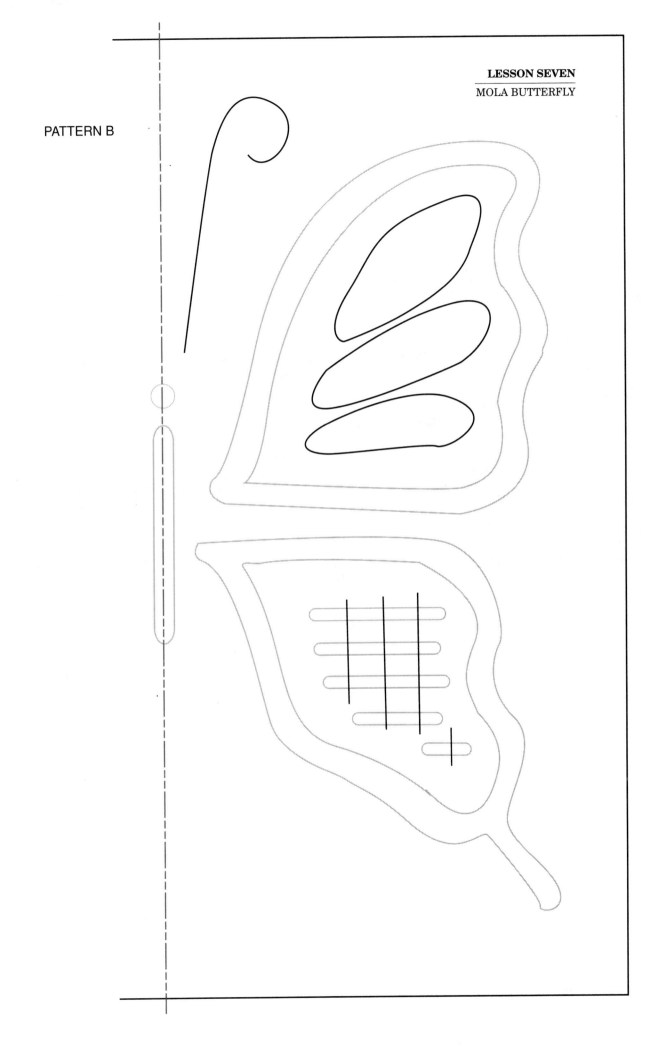

PATTERN B

HOW ARE YOU DOING?

When you have finished your blocks, check them to see how well you are doing.

SPECIFIC TECHNIQUES:

Hawaiian Applique

• Applique should lie flat on the block and not be puffy or puckered. Use care in unfolding cut fabric and arranging on the background block. Baste carefully and thoroughly on a flat surface.

• There should not be any raw edges escaping from the applique. In areas where the seam allowance is very small, such as inside points and small curves, stitches should be smaller and closer together to control the edge.

• Curves should be smoothly shaped. It takes practice to use the needle to turn under a consistent seam allowance without points or puckers.

• Points should be sharp. Be sure to take an extra stitch to hold the point down as you turn under the edge. Fold all of the fabric of the point under the applique so no raw edges are visible. Take an long extra stitch to visually sharpen the point as described in Lesson 4, Pattern C.

Pa Ndau

• Channels should be an even width. Stitching under the second edge is the critical point. Be careful not to clip too far into curves and not to turn under too much on straight sections.

• Curves should be smooth. Close clipping on the inside curves helps, about $1/16$" apart. Use your thumbnail to hold the edge in place for stitching.

• Raw edges should not show. Be sure to turn under clipped areas carefully to capture all the threads. Stitch closely at the ends of the channels.

Chintz Applique

•Applied pieces should lie flat, with no puckering. Pin or baste carefully in place.

•Raw edges should not show. Use small, close stitching on inside points and curves.

Mola

•Channels should be even in width. Stitch the second edge carefully. Also, be careful not to turn under too much seam allowance on the bumps of the scallops, which will flatten them out.

•Raw edges should not show. Be especially careful in the small curves, and use small close stitching.

GENERAL APPEARANCE:

•Blocks should lie flat and not be distorted by the applique. Be sure that you are not drawing up the stitch too tight, and that layers are basted firmly so you won't displace them as you stitch.

LECTURE: QUILTING TODAY

Since the American Bicentennial renewed interest in quilting in 1976, the growth has been phenomenal. In the United States, contemporary quilters who developed new techniques or design approaches, or were skilled in color theory began to travel around the country, sharing their skills and ideas with others. Major quilt exhibits and competitions drew thousands of visitors, inspiring many to investigate the craft. A virtual explosion of publications – how-to books, collections of work in specific techniques, historical documentation, consumer magazines – is making it possible for even isolated quilters to participate fully.

Quilters don't seem to stay isolated very long, however. Organizations are available to everyone, from local informal groups to those on an international scale. (More about them is included in the next lecture.) It also didn't take long for the interest to spread to other areas of the world. Although American quilting may have been imitated in the beginning, each country soon used its own heritage, traditions, and interests to develop quilting in its own way. Quilters in England, Australia, New Zealand, Japan, and a number of other countries have organized guilds and held major conferences. Tours and exchange programs between the various countries result in personal friendships around the world.

Another exciting development in today's quilt world is the growing interest in historical documentation of existing quilts. The Kentucky Heritage Quilt Project was among the first, and led the way for many state and area projects that have followed. At Quilt Discovery Days, area residents are invited to bring family quilts to be photographed and have an oral history taken. The information accumulated will be useful to the growing field of quilt historians, who are researching many aspects of the importance of quilting in the lives of our mothers and grandmothers.

Home Study Course
in
Quiltmaking

LESSON EIGHT
Trapunto And Shadow Applique

Pattern A: Heart Ring (Shadow Applique)
Beginner Level

Pattern B: **Rose in Full Bloom** (Trapunto)
Intermediate Level

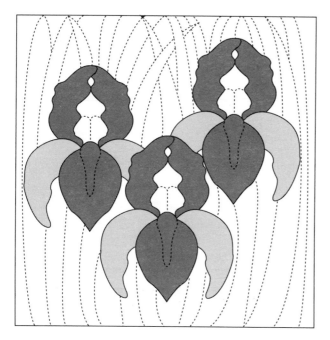

Pattern C: Iris Garden (Shadow Applique)
Advanced Level

Pattern D: **Ring of Roses** (Cording)
Challenge Level

LESSON EIGHT: TRAPUNTO AND SHADOW APPLIQUE

To use this lesson, first read its Introduction. If you are making the wallhanging, decide which pattern you would like to make. Each one has the difficulty level indicated so that you can take into account your own skills, interest, and time. If you are making the full-size quilt, you will want to complete all of the blocks.

Note: If you want to construct a top and use a frame to baste and quilt, see Lesson Ten: Section Two; then go on to Lesson Eight.

INTRODUCTION TO TRAPUNTO AND SHADOW QUILTING

This lesson covers two ways to add interest to designs made with the quilting stitch, one very old way and the other of contemporary origin. You've already learned about background grids, symmetrical design, and realistic patterns in previous lessons. Two of the blocks in this lesson use trapunto to enhance the quilted design, and two use shadow quilting to define the quilted shapes.

Trapunto

The word *trapunto* usually refers to the process of adding additional stuffing to selected areas of the quilted design. There is often debate as to whether this is the proper term to refer to this technique. Some people feel that it refers only to one method of raising a design, and the broad term should be *stuffed work*. I am in favor of more colorful words and realize that language is constantly changing. I like the word "trapunto" (pronounce it either tra-pun´-to or tra-poon´-to) and use it in preference to "stuffed work" which has a variety of unpleasant connotations (stuffy people, stuffy noses, etc.).

Trapunto is a very old technique. The oldest existing example of quilting is a series of three pieces from Sicily done around 1400 as a wedding gift for an aristocrat. These works tell the story of Tristan and Isolde, and the figures are enhanced with stuffing and cording.

Trapunto is so time-consuming and painstaking that its presence indicates the availability of leisure to do it or the money to hire someone else to do it. It was used frequently in Europe to decorate court clothing and for fine infants' and ladies' wear.

In America, when families acquired enough wealth so women could afford a whole piece of fabric for a quilt and could sit in the parlor all day and do needlework, patterns were designed whose effect depended solely on quilting and stuffing. These "white work" quilts were often the crowning achievement of a woman's needlework experience, and took a minimum of a year to complete.

Shadow Applique

I'm not sure how the idea for shadow applique occurred. Perhaps it was an attempt to imitate the effect of using colored yarn for trapunto, a technique developed by Marge Murphy and Nancy Donahue, or perhaps to find a simple substitute for traditional applique to add areas of color to a quilt top. At any rate, layering the background, colorful fabric shapes, and cotton voile or organdy, and then quilting with batting and backing results in a soft, pastel version of a quilt block.

Shadow applique is often used for children's clothing, or to add a feminine look to yokes or vests. One of the technique's most enthusiastic supporters is Marjorie Puckett, who has designed a number of projects for major pattern companies.

Since each of the blocks in this lesson uses a different approach, there are no general instructions.

RESOURCES

Trapunto, Mary Morgan and Dee Mosteller, Charles Scribner's Sons, New York, NY, 1977.
Quilting, Patchwork, Applique, and Trapunto, Thelma R. Newman, Crown Publishers, Inc., New York, NY 1974.

Pattern A: **Heart Ring** (Shadow Applique), *Beginner Level*

This block uses a layer of voile to soften the colors of the designs, and the background quilting pattern highlights the shapes.

STEP 1:

a: Trace the full-size pattern. Mark a 10" square on a background block. Trace the placement of the hearts and center circle on the background block.

b: Prewash the cotton voile to soften it and remove the sizing. Cut an 11" square and mark a 10" square on it, using the template. Trace the quilting pattern on the voile block. Since the weave of the voile is very open, you will need to use a soft pencil for marking. Make the marks just dark enough to be seen.

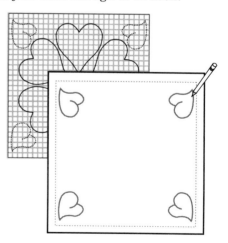

STEP 2:

Since it is not necessary to indicate a stitching line on the shadow shapes, you can cut them all at one time if you have very sharp fabric scissors. Trace the heart shape on a piece of typing paper and cut out. Pin it to six layers of fabric and then carefully cut around the paper pattern. The grain line should be parallel to the center line of the heart.

The center circle is 1", the same size as the circles for the grapes in Lesson Four, Pattern D. You can use the template from that lesson, or if you don't have one, trace the circle from the Heart Ring pattern and make a template.

To avoid fraying the edges of the shapes before they are stitched, handle them very carefully and as little as possible.

STEP 3:

Working on a flat surface, spread out the background block. Position the heart shapes and the center circle as indicated by the traced pattern. Carefully lay the voile over the background and hearts, matching the marked seam lines. Pin through the hearts and circle to hold the layers in place until they are basted.

STEP 4:

Continuing to work on a flat surface, spread out the backing and batting, and position the background block. Baste around the seam lines of the background block; then baste a circle where the edges of the hearts meet. Add diagonal lines of basting through each pair of hearts.

STEP 5:

Quilt around the center circle and the hearts, using contrasting colored thread. Quilt the leaf designs with matching thread.

If you have been taking very tiny stitches in quilting other blocks, you may need to make them larger to hold the voile, since the weave is so open. If the edges of the shadow shapes have frayed, tuck the loose ends back in as you quilt.

Pattern B: **Rose in Full Bloom** (Trapunto), *Intermediate Level*

The traditional method of cutting slits in the back of the fabric to add stuffing ruins the back of a piece and requires a lining. Lola Choinski developed this method which takes a little longer, but lets the quilt stitching show on the back.

STEP 1:

Trace the pattern. Mark a 10" square on a background block, using the prepared template. Trace the rose and leaves on the front of the block.

STEP 2:

a: Cut an 11" square of cotton voile (or other very lightweight fabric) and baste to the back of the block around the seam lines.

b: Using small stitches, baste just inside the marked lines of each section of the rose, making an enclosed shape. Do not knot ends of basting threads and cut thread when you change directions. This makes the basting stitches easier to remove.

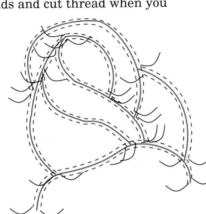

STEP 3:

When the basting is complete, turn the block over. Starting in the center of the block, make a small slit through the voile in the center of an enclosed shape. Use sharp embroidery scissors, and be careful not to cut through the top layer. Gently insert soft stuffing. Use a broken bamboo skewer or an orange stick. *Do not overstuff.* You can always add more. Stuffing should feel soft, not hard or lumpy. Don't try to fill the entire shape with one piece of batting. Use just a little at a time. Be especially careful about over-stuffing the larger shapes. Long, narrow shapes may need more than one slit.

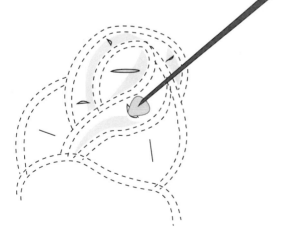

Hint:
Frequently stop and pull on the grain of the block in both directions to check on whether it is being distorted by the stuffing.

STEP 4:

Baste the stuffed block to the backing and batting, around the edges and diagonally from corner to corner.

Quilt on the pattern lines, between the lines of basting, removing the basting as you go. Use a contrasting thread. Quilt the background leaves and veins, using a matching thread.

Suggested quilting design

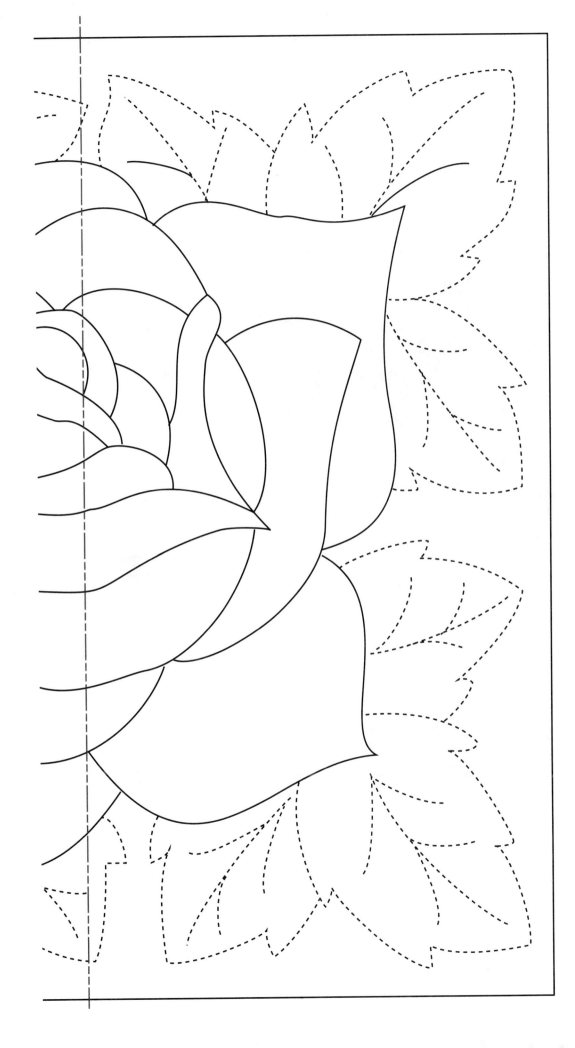

Pattern C: **Iris Garden** (Shadow Applique), *Advanced Level*

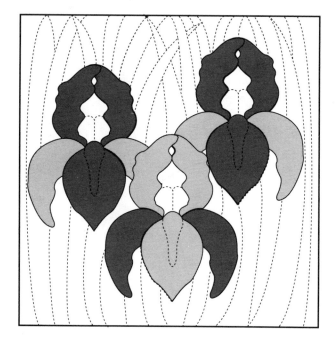

This block uses a layer of voile to soften the colors of the design and the background quilting pattern highlights the shapes.

STEP 1:

a: Trace the pattern. Mark a 10" square on a piece of background fabric. Trace the placement of the flowers on the background block.

b: Prewash the cotton voile to soften it and remove the sizing. Cut an 11" square and mark a 10" square on it. Trace the quilting pattern on the voile block. Since the weave of the voile is very open, you will need to use a soft pencil for marking. Make the marks just dark enough to see.

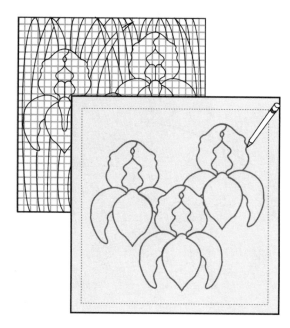

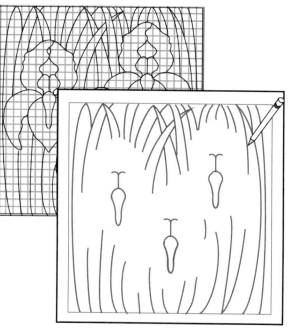

STEP 2:

Prepare three templates from the center flower on the pattern; use the upper-left petal, the lower left petal, and the central-lower petal. All the shadow shapes will be cut the same and trimmed after they have been placed on the background.

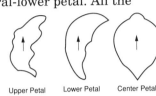

Upper Petal   Lower Petal   Center Petal

STEP 3:

If you are using two fabrics, cut shapes as follows:

Two upper petals and two reversed from Fabric A
One upper petal and one reversed from Fabric B
One lower petal and one reversed from Fabric A
Two lower petals and two reversed from Fabric B
Two center petals from Fabric A
One center petal from Fabric B

Grain lines should go in the long direction of each shape. Handle the shapes very carefully after cutting, to keep them from fraying before they are stitched.

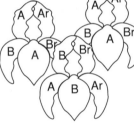

STEP 4:

Working on a flat surface, lay out the background block, and start with the left-hand flower. Place the upper right petal in position; then place the upper left petal over it. Mark the overlap line, then trim the right petal and replace. Place the rest of the petals for that flower in position.

Proceed similarly for the

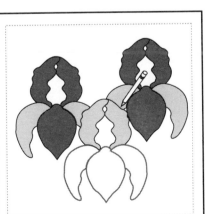

right-hand flower, trimming the upper right petal at the overlap. Place the petals for the central flower, marking and trimming the overlap on the left- and right-hand flowers, as well as the upper petal.

When you are finished, shapes should not overlap, but barely touch. Lay the voile over the top with the quilting lines in the correct position. Keeping the block flat, baste with long stitches through all of the shadow shapes.

STEP 5:

Lay the backing and batting on a flat surface, and position the basted background block. Baste along the seam lines, then diagonally from corner to corner. Add a line of basting horizontally and vertically through each flower.

Quilt around the iris shadow shapes, adding the detail at the same time, using contrasting thread. Then add the background leaves. If you have been taking very tiny stitches in quilting other blocks, you may need to make them larger to hold the voile, since the weave is so open. If the edges of the shadow shapes have frayed, tuck the loose ends back in as you quilt.

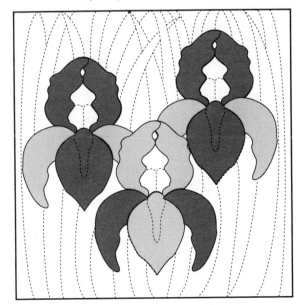

Suggested quilting design

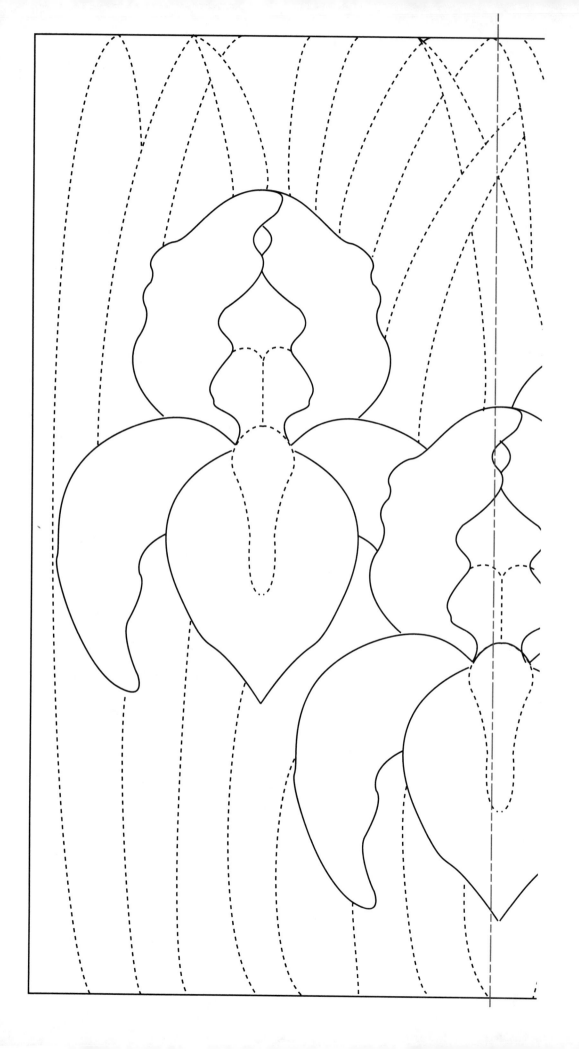

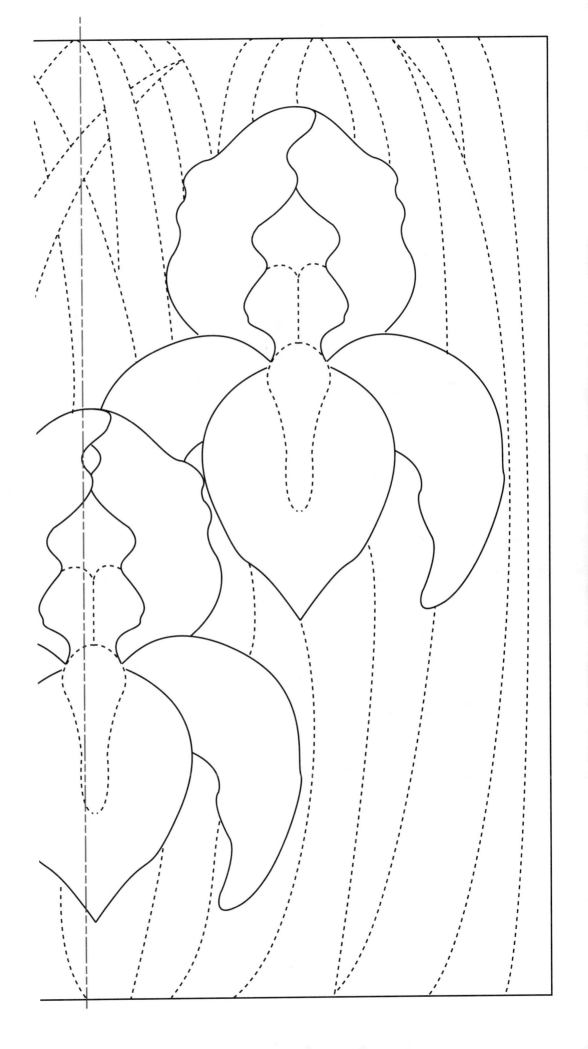

Pattern D: **Ring of Roses** (Cording), *Challenge Level*

In this version of adding stuffing to the quilted design, the stitching is completed first; then yarn is carefully pulled through the stuffed areas.

STEP 1:

Trace the pattern. Mark a 10" square on a background block. Trace the quilting design on the block.

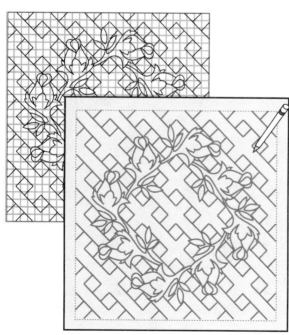

STEP 2:

Baste the block to the backing and batting.

STEP 3:

Quilt the ring of roses in a contrasting color thread and the background basket-weave in a matching thread.

STEP 4:

Add yarn to the shaded areas in the diagram.

a: Thread a tapestry needle with a short length of yarn. The yarn should be doubled. From the back of the quilted block, carefully insert the needle between the layers in an area to be stuffed (indicated by shading in the accompanying diagram.) Bring the needle out at the far edge of the shape; then pull the yarn through just to the tail.

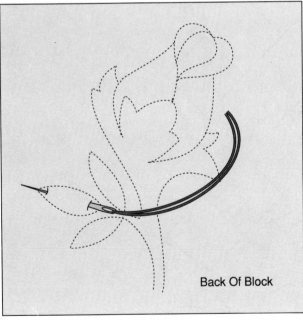

Back Of Block

b: Clip the yarn (carefully!). Then use the point of the needle to pull it completely into the shape so it disappears.

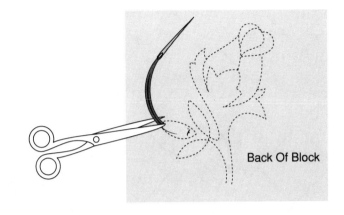

Back Of Block

c: Use your fingernail to "scratch" the hole closed. The leaves and stems should be adequately stuffed with one double yarn, but the bottom of the bud will require parallel lengths of yarn to fill it.

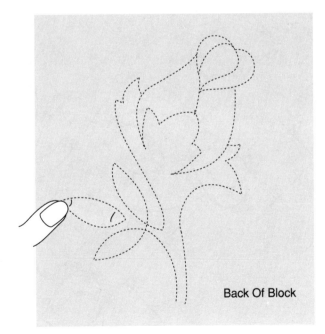

Back Of Block

Repeat for the remaining roses.

Hint:
Stop frequently and pull on the grain of the block in both directions to work the stuffing into the design and to make sure it is not distorted.

HOW ARE YOU DOING?

When you have finished your blocks, check them to see how well you are doing.

Shadow Applique:

• Applique shapes should lie smoothly. Be sure to work on a flat surface when you baste the layers together.

• Voile should lie flat and not be distorted. Be sure to add enough basting before quilting.

• Quilting stitches should be large enough to catch the threads of the voile firmly.

Trapunto:

• Stuffing should be soft. Start with a very small amount and then add more if necessary.

• Stuffing should be smooth, not lumpy. Insert very small amounts each time. Try different stuffing implements, some with rough, instead of smooth, surfaces. Don't jam the stuffing into the far corners, but rather work it in gently.

• The block should not be distorted. Overstuffing is the major cause of distortion. Remove some of the stuffing.

• Needle holes from the cording process should not show. Use a needle with a blunt point to avoid breaking threads. Scratch the holes closed with a fingernail.

LECTURE: QUILT COMPETITIONS

Since the first major quilt contest of the recent revival, held in 1976 in Warren, Michigan, the quality of the technical skills of quiltmakers has risen dramatically. Not only have the piecing, applique, and quilting improved, but the visual impact of many pieces is breathtaking. I feel that in large part this is due to the evaluations quilters receive from judges in competition.

If you are a new quilter learning the skills by working through the lessons in this Home Study Course, you may well be intimidated by the idea of submitting quilts to be judged, feeling that there is no way you can compete with experienced practitioners. I can sympathize with that feeling, but I'd also like to encourage you to enter judged events as soon as you feel ready. In fact, some shows even have a special category for "First Quilt" so that beginners can get their feet wet in competition.

Let me tell you a little bit about quilt contests, so that you will understand how they work. When a sponsoring organization decides to have a quilt contest, one of the first things they do is develop an entry form which interested quilters can send for. There is usually a fee for entering the contest, which helps pay for printing, exhibition expenses, and judges. The entry form will list various categories quilters can enter their quilt in, dividing entries by such factors as technique and size. The number of possible categories depends on the size of the show, but quilts are usually separated into large and small sizes (with specific measurements given), and into pieced, applique, mixed-technique, and all-quilted. Some shows also separate hand and machine quilting, and divide the entrants by skill level. The quilt you complete with the Home Study Course lessons would be entered in a mixed-technique category, because it contains both piecing and applique. Some shows may also ask for a slide of the quilt you are entering, either to assist them in arranging the hanging or to do preliminary jurying of the entries.

The information accompanying the entry form will tell you where and when to ship your quilt. Pack your quilt very carefully, in a cloth bag and then in a plastic bag, and use a sturdy box. Do not mark "quilt" on the outside of the box. Be sure to include a slip inside the box identifying your quilt and containing the name and address you are shipping it to, and your name and address. You can also include a return postcard for the entry chairman to send back to you so that you know it arrived. Insure it for a realistic value. If the quilt is lost in transit, you will only be reimbursed the cost of the materials unless you have had it appraised. The American Quilter's Society, Box 3290, Paducah, KY 42002-3290 can provide a list of certified appraisers.

After all the entries have arrived at the show site, they will be judged. There may be one to four judges, selected by the show sponsors. They will examine each entry and agree on the ribbon winners for each category, and usually a "Best of Show" as well. Many exhibits also ask viewers to vote on their favorite quilt, giving the winner a "Viewers' Choice" award.

For each lesson in this Home Study Course, I have provided a "How Are You Doing?" checklist for your technical skills. Each of the points listed are examined by judges when they assess the workmanship of a quilt. In addition, most judges are equally concerned with the visual impact, which includes how the quilt looks from a distance, the colors and fabrics used, the scale and unity of the design, and any story it might tell.

When you are ready to send a quilt to a competition, you will find that judges' comments are not the only benefit you receive. You will also be part of a process that draws others into exploring the world of quilting, because they can see first-hand how beautiful the results are, and what a wide range of techniques and messages quilts can involve. Attending the show to see what others are doing will be enjoyable, especially if you stand by your entry for a while and talk to people about it. You'll be delighted by the positive feedback, even if you don't manage to win a ribbon.

Home Study Course
in
Quiltmaking

LESSON NINE
Contemporary Applique

Pattern A: Rolling Hills (Landscape Applique)
Beginner Level

Pattern B: Love Birds (Cut-away Applique)
Intermediate Level

Pattern C: Blossom Beauty (Stained Glass)
Advanced Level

Pattern D: Celtic Rose
Challenge Level

LESSON NINE: CONTEMPORARY APPLIQUE

To use this lesson, first read its Introduction. If you are making the wallhanging, decide which pattern you would like to make. Each one has the difficulty level indicated so that you can take into account your own skills, interest, and time. If you are making the full-size quilt, you will want to complete all of the blocks.

Note: If you want to construct a top and use a frame to baste and quilt, see Lesson Ten: Section Two.

INTRODUCTION TO
CONTEMPORARY APPLIQUE

Several contemporary quiltmakers have developed distinctive applique styles which do not resemble traditional techniques and are fun to learn. Jo Diggs has used simple curved shapes to give the impression of landscapes. Margot Carter Blair marks the pattern on the applique fabric and then cuts it away as she is working, in a method reminiscent of Mola technique. Roberta Horton developed the Stained Glass style of applique when the class she was teaching decided they would like to duplicate that technique in fabric. Philomena Wiechec used designs from her Welch heritage to develop the Celtic-style bias applique.

The methods presented here are not necessarily the ones taught by these quilters, but, rather are ones based on their ideas.

Since each of the blocks in this lesson uses a different approach, there are no general instructions.

RESOURCE

Celtic Quilt Designs, adapted by Philomena Wiechec, Celtic Design Co., Saratoga, CA, 1980.

Pattern A: **Rolling Hills** (Landscape Applique), *Beginner Level*

Softly curved shapes appliqued to a background give the illusion of a landscape, in a pattern similar to those of Jo Diggs.

STEP 1:

Trace the pattern if desired. Much of the charm of this technique is in freehand cutting and placement of fabric, so you are encouraged to develop your own design. If you use the pattern included, lightly mark the top of the hills and the outside cloud shape on the background block.

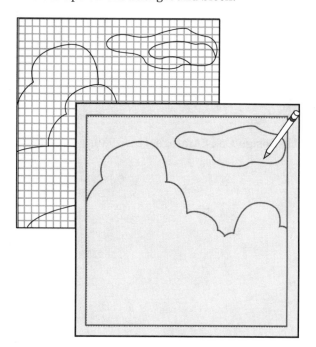

STEP 2:

Cut the paper pattern apart. Pin the pieces to the right side of the fabric, right side up, and cut the shapes out with a generous ¼" seam allowance. If you are cutting shapes freehand, make sure that any overlaps in the pieces are at least ½" to allow for turning under ¼" on the edges. In general, the grain lines of the shapes should follow the grain line of the background block, but experiment with bias grain lines for a different texture if you wish.

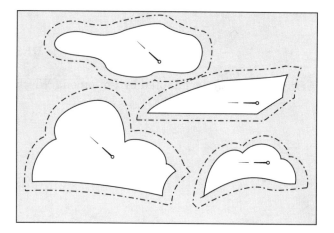

STEP 3:

Pin the fabric pieces to the background block. Rearrange, trim, change fabrics or add more pieces until you are pleased with the design. Remember that pieces must overlap by at least ½" to allow turning under.

STEP 4:

Start at the top of the design and applique the shapes farthest back first. Do not turn under any edges that will be covered by another shape, or the edges on the outside of the block. Use your needle to smoothly turn under the ¼" on the raw

edges to be stitched as you work. Clip into inside points. When placing a shape over one already stitched down, be sure that you overlap the edges at least ½", so there won't be a gap when you turn under ¼".

Hint:

If you are using light-colored fabrics in your applique, you may need to trim darker ones from behind them to avoid shadowing. See Lesson Four, Pattern D, STEP 6.

STEP 5:

When all shapes have been appliqued, baste the completed block to the backing and batting.

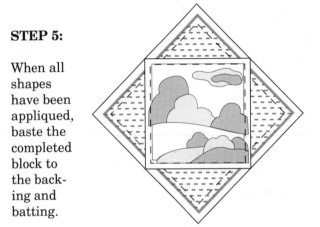

Quilt around the edges of the shapes by hand or by machine.

Suggested quilting design

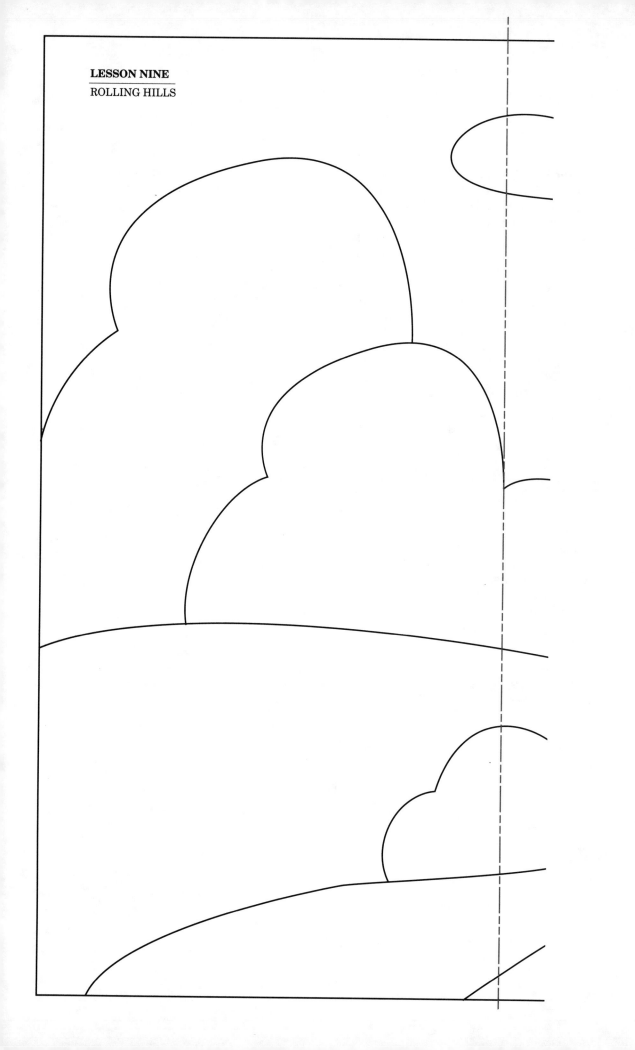

Pattern B: **Love Birds** (Cut-away Applique), *Intermediate Level*

The design for this cut-away applique pattern was inspired by Polish paper cutting. The technique gives you greater control over the many bias edges.

STEP 1:

Trace the pattern. Mark the bird pattern on Fabric A, including the block seam lines. Cut it out as a rectangle, using the seam lines.

Trace the winged heart pattern on Fabric B, including the block seam lines, and cut it out as a rectangle, using the seam lines. Use a light box if necessary.

Mark a 10" square on a background block.

STEP 2:

Baste the bird fabric to the background block, matching the cut edges with the top and side seam lines. Baste outside the edges of the bird shapes.

STEP 3:

a: Begin stitching at the bottom of the bird's feet in the center. Cut away the outside edge for about 1", leaving a generous ⅛" seam allowance. Clip inside curves almost to the marked line. Turn the seam allowance with the needle, making sure the marked line is turned completely under. Stitch about ½", then cut another 1" and continue stitching. Continue in this fashion until you get to the bottom of the other foot.

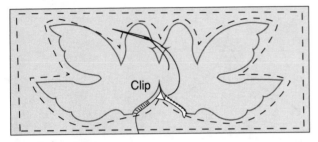

b: Start on the outside of the bird shape at the bottom edge in the same way. Clip the inside points almost to the marked line. Work carefully on the wing and tail scallops to curve them smoothly.

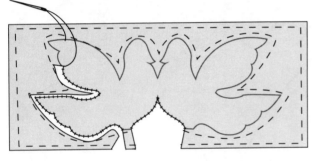

At the outside points, stitch up to the end of the point; then take an extra stitch to hold it securely. Use the needle to tuck the excess fabric under the edge and hold it with small stitches. Work carefully on the bird beaks to keep them sharp.

Hint:
Use a long stitch on the point to extend it visually as in Lesson Four, Pattern C, STEP 5b.

c. When the birds have been completed, remove the basting stitches and excess fabric.

STEP 4:

Baste the rectangle for the winged heart in place. Be sure the top edge overlaps the birds' feet by at least ½". Baste around the outside of the heart shape and the outside of the inner heart.

STEP 5:

a: Begin stitching in the inner heart along a long edge. Clip Fabric B carefully to start the cutting line, ⅛" inside the marked line. Do not cut through the background block.

b: Cut and stitch the outer heart.

STEP 6:

Mark the triple heart quilting design in the corners of the block.

Baste the completed block to the backing and batting.

Quilt just outside the edges of the applique. Quilt the triple heart design.

Suggested quilting design

LESSON NINE
LOVE BIRDS

LESSON NINE
LOVE BIRDS

Pattern C: **Blossom Beauty** (Stained Glass), *Advanced Level*

To imitate the effect of Stained Glass, fabric shapes are basted to the background block and the raw edges are covered by a bias strip. The inner edge of the bias is stitched first, and then the outer edge is stretched into position.

Be careful not to stretch the bias too much or it will distort the block. Ease it slightly into the inner curves.

STEP 1:

Trace the pattern. Mark a 10" square on a background block, and then mark the pattern on the block.

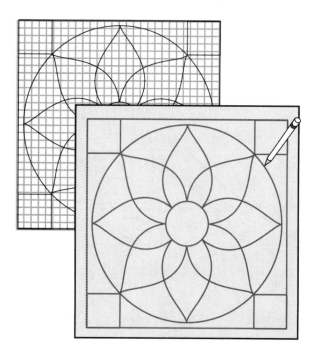

STEP 2:

Make a template for each of the shapes in the pattern, adding ¼" seam allowance to two sides of the square. Fabric may be layered to cut four squares and eight of each remaining shape. Grain lines should be parallel to the longest dimension of the templates.

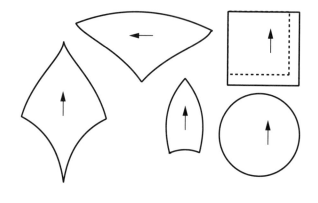

STEP 3:

Baste the fabric shapes in place on the background block. Edges should meet but not overlap.

STEP 4:

Cut a 12" square of fabric for bias strips. Cut the square in half diagonally, and stitch the opposite edges together to form a parallelogram. Mark and cut ¾" wide strips. Fold strips in thirds and baste down the center.

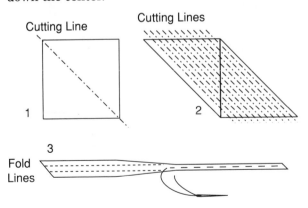

STEP 5:

a: Start stitching along an inner curve of a petal, beginning at the edge of the center circle. Lay a bias strip along the curve, covering the raw edges of both fabrics. Applique the inner curve, then the outer curve, making sure to catch the edges of the basted shapes in the stitching.

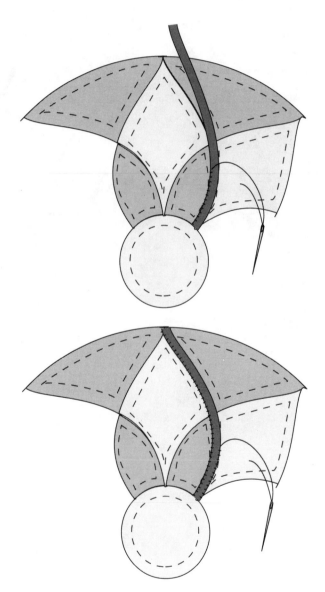

Trim the bias strip even with the edge of the outer circle.

b: Stitch the opposite side of the petal.

STEP 6:

Using the same technique, cover the edges of the corner squares. The bias strip should extend into the seam allowances of the block. Trim the ends even with the edge of the outer circle.

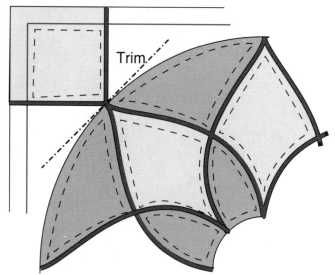

STEP 7:

a: Stitch a bias strip to the inner circle, beginning with the inner curve. Leave about 1" of bias free at the start, and stop stitching 1" from the end. Remove basting from the free ends of the bias; unfold and join strips in a diagonal seam. Refold and continue stitching the inner curve.

Stitch the outer curve, making sure to completely cover the ends of the petal pieces.

b: Stitch the outer circle, beginning on the inner curve as above, and stitching the ends in the same manner. Make sure the ends of each petal are completely covered. Stitch the outer curve, trimming the ends of petals if necessary.

c: Remove the basting stitches.

STEP 8:

Baste completed block to batting and backing.

Quilt around the outer circle and the corner squares.

Suggested quilting design

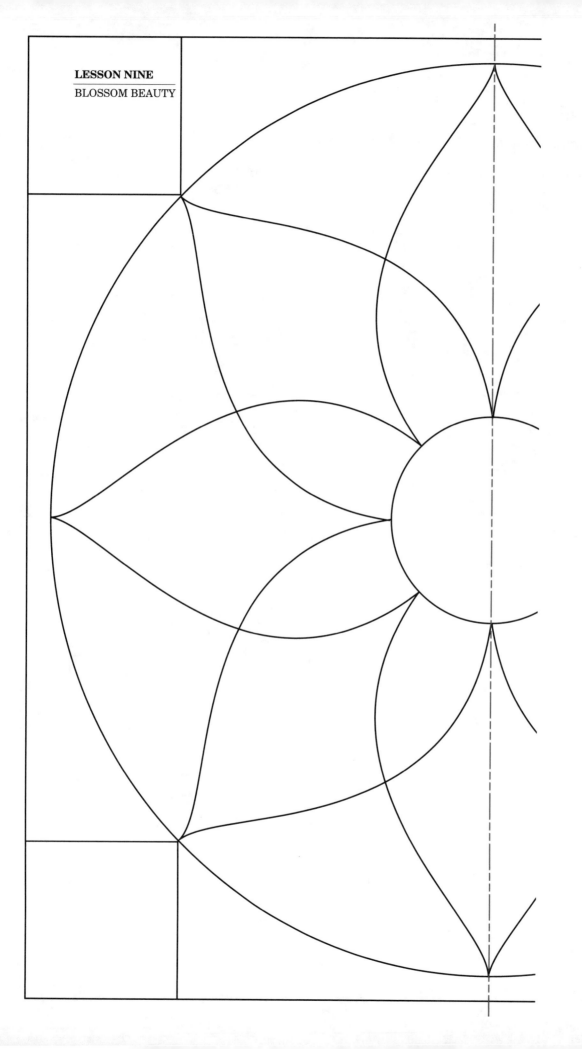

LESSON NINE
BLOSSOM BEAUTY

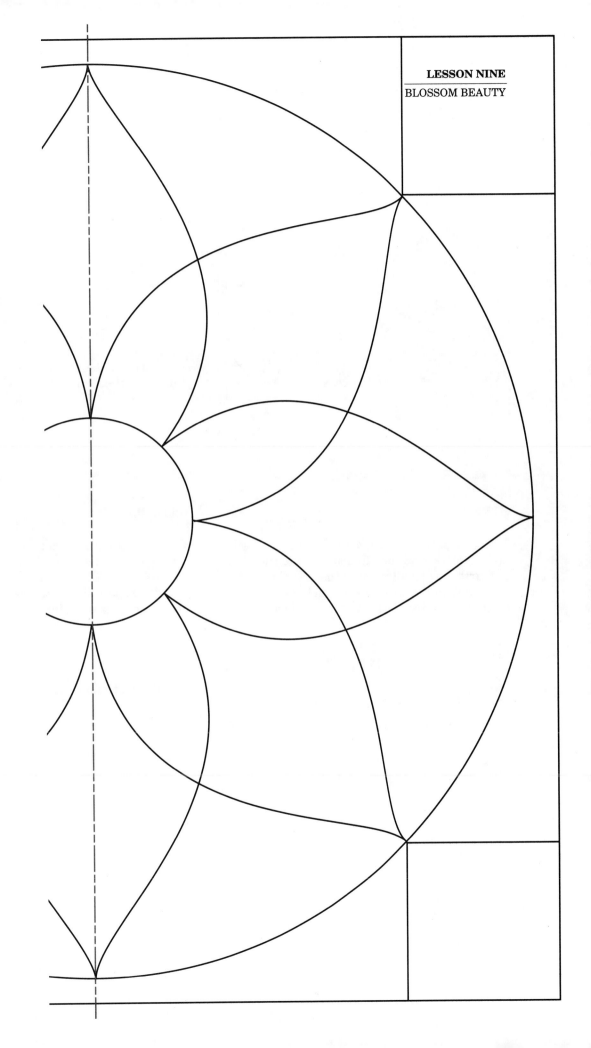

Pattern D: **Celtic Rose**, *Challenge Level*

Although this design also uses bias strips of fabric, as in the Stained Glass technique, the strips go over and under each other in a three-dimensional effect. Each section of design uses one strip of bias which alternately goes over and under itself. The challenge is to get all the overs and unders in the right places.

STEP 1:

Trace the pattern. Mark a 10" square on a background block, and then fold and crease the block in fourths diagonally. Match the dotted line of the pattern with the creases and mark the background. Then rotate the pattern to mark each side in turn.

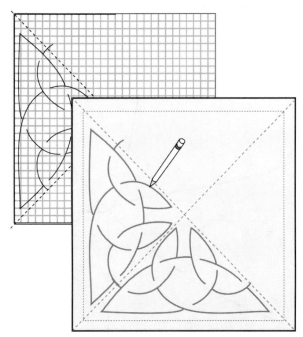

STEP 2:

Cut a 15" square to make bias strips. Cut it in half diagonally, and then seam the straight edges to make a parallelogram as in Pattern C. Mark 1¼" strips parallel to the top edge, and then seam the remaining straight edges to make a tube. At the seam, match the marked lines to the next line down, so that when you cut on the line, it will be a continuous strip.

Cut the continuous strip and then cut it into four equal pieces. Press each section in half and

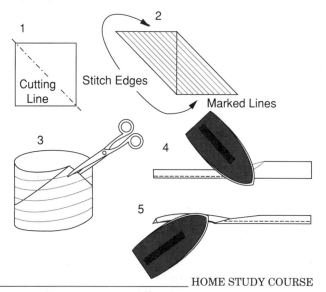

machine stitch ⅛" from the raw edges. Fold in half again and press, stretching the second folded edge to form a slight curve.

STEP 3:

a: Stitch one section of pattern at a time. Be careful not to stretch the bias too much, or the background block will be distorted. Begin at the left edge of the pattern where the bias goes "under." Use a small applique stitch to stitch the second folded edge to the marked line. Stitch as far as the gap, add an extra stitch to hold the bias firmly, then slip the needle under the block to skip the gap and resume stitching.

Hint:
Put a safety pin at each gap in the pattern line to remind you not to stitch it down.

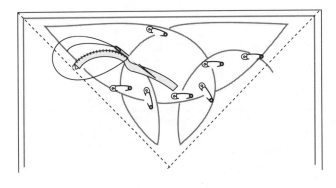

b: Continue stitching to the point. Take extra stitches to hold the point firmly. Next, fold the bias and continue stitching up the other side. Use a small safety pin in the end of the bias to slip it through the first gap you left.

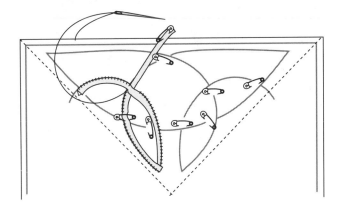

c: Continue stitching to the end of your thread.

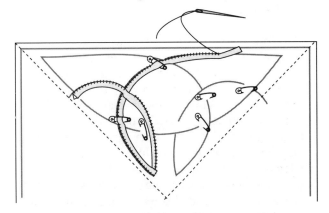

d: Go back to the beginning of the bias and stitch the second edge, gently easing it in place around the curves. Do not stitch gaps closed yet. Stop about 1" from the point.

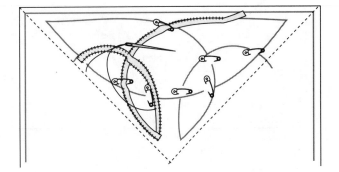

e: Fold the top of the bias out of the way, and trim the under fold so it will lie flat in the point. Trim a small triangle out of the top fold, with the point about 1/16" from the edge. Fold the top over the bottom (note diagram for direction of fold), and stitch the edge. At the

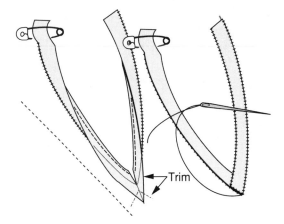

Trim

bottom, tuck under the remaining raw edge and stitch.

f: Continue stitching down the second edge of the bias. When you reach a spot where the bias goes "under," stitch down both sides of the top bias before continuing. Continue to stitch, alternating sides of bias, until you reach the end of the quarter pattern. Stitch both edges of the bias to just inside the "under" gap in the next quarter pattern. Trim the bias end. The raw edge of the next bias strip should just meet the previous bias. Ends will be covered as the motif is stitched. The end of the last bias strip tucks under the gap in the first quarter pattern. Stitch the top edge over it.

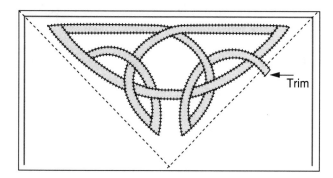

STEP 4:

Baste the completed block to batting and backing.

Quilt around the edges of the bias strips.

Suggested quilting design

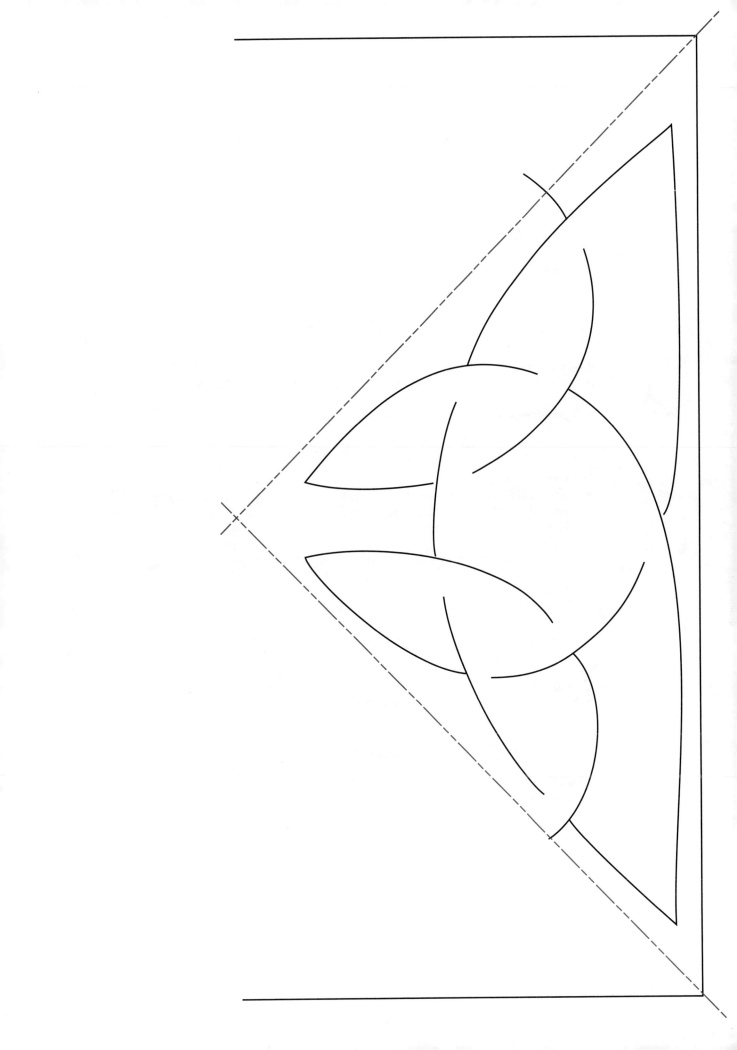

HOW ARE YOU DOING?

When you have finished your blocks, check them to see how well you are doing.

Rolling Hills:
- Curves should be smoothly shaped. If you have little points on your outside curves, turn under less seam allowance. If your inside curves pucker, clip them more closely.

- Raw edges should not be visible, especially in inside points. Stitch more closely.

Love Birds:
- Scallops should be even and smooth. Be careful turning under the edges.

- Raw edges should not show. Close, tight stitches will help.

- Inside curves should be smooth. Clip closely before turning.

Blossom Beauty:
- Bias should cover the raw edges completely. Tuck them under the bias strips far enough to hold them securely, or, if necessary, remove stitching and make the bias a little wider.

- Raw ends of bias should be covered completely. Trim before stitching inner and outer circle.

- Bias width should be consistent.

- The end joins in the inner and outer circle should be smooth.

Celtic Rose:
- Bias should lie flat and not distort the background. Be careful not to stretch it while stitching.

- Curves should be smoothly shaped. Press a curve into the bias before using it.

- Points should appear sharp. They will be very bulky, so work carefully, and be sure all raw edges are stitched under.

- The raw ends of the bias should be hidden at an underlap.

LECTURE: WHERE DO YOU GO FROM HERE?

Contacting Other Quilters

If you have been working through the Home Study Course on your own, without contact with other quilters, it's time to find some. There are many benefits to joining a quilt group or starting one of your own. There are groups which range from neighborhood stitch-and-sew sessions, to area or state-wide groups, all the way up to several national or international organizations. The first thing to do is to find out whether any such groups are available in your area. One way to do that is to attend a nearby (or even state-wide) quilt show, and ask a member of the sponsoring organization about members or groups in your area. Another way is to visit the closest quilt shop and make similar inquiries. Don't be shy about calling the person whose name you are given; most quilt groups welcome new members, especially beginners, and most quilters are eager to make new friends with the same interest.

Contact with other quilters will not only expand your knowledge of the possibilities of quilting, but will also give you enthusiasm to help you through difficult spots in your work, provide technical help if you get stuck, and applaud your result when it is finished. If there are no convenient groups nearby, start one yourself. Put a notice in the local paper or church bulletin, or in the state guild newsletter. Even six or eight people who get together informally once a month will have a good time doing it, and you'll have someone to talk to who understands the language.

Home Study Course
in
Quiltmaking

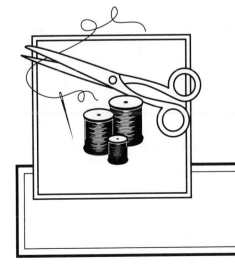

LESSON TEN
The Finishing Touch

LESSON TEN: THE FINISHING TOUCH

SECTION ONE: Making a Quilt with the Quilted Blocks

The first section of this lesson covers putting the quilted blocks together, then adding and quilting the border. If you want to construct a top and use a frame to baste and quilt, Section Two gives the instructions.

STEP 1:

The first step in finishing is arranging the blocks. Find an area large enough to lay them all out in order, so you can step back and look at the quilt as a whole. If you are making the full-size quilt, a clear floor area is best. If you can't get far enough away to see how the blocks relate to each other, look at them through a camera lens or the wrong end of a pair of binoculars.

In the full-size quilt, rows of constructed (pieced or appliqued) blocks alternate with rows of blocks with quilted patterns. *If you have done one block from each lesson to make a wallhanging, arrange the blocks as shown, with the block from Lesson Eight in one of the single rows.*

You will probably want to include the setting squares when you lay out the blocks so you can see how the whole quilt looks together.

STEP 2:

Blocks in a sampler quilt must be arranged with care so the entire quilt is balanced and looks like a unit. Bright colors need to be evenly distributed, and it looks more natural to have lighter colors near the top and darker colors near the bottom. Each fabric should also be somewhat balanced, at least across a line of vertical symmetry.

Design elements should also be balanced. Strong diagonals, circular motifs, and naturalistic patterns should not cluster in one area. Also, since Sunbonnet Sally and Overall Sam are the only blocks with figures, and Heart Ring and Iris Garden are the only Shadow Applique blocks, they should be balanced.

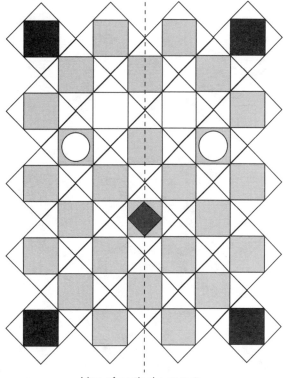

Line of vertical symmetry

When you have determined the most pleasing arrangement of your blocks, safety pin the edges of the backing blocks together until you are ready to stitch them.

STEP 3:

Cut 11½" setting squares; 31 for the quilt, 7 for the wallhanging. If you have delayed purchasing and cutting the setting block fabric to this point, now is the time to decide on what will enhance the blocks of your quilt. Perhaps a large-scale print in soft colors, or a textured-looking print, or even a darker fabric to contrast with the fabrics you have used.

Advanced quilters might want to consider using stripes as I did, constructing the setting squares of four triangles. Experiment with which way the pattern runs.

Quilters looking for a challenge could duplicate the flat piping and border on the setting squares that I used on my quilt. If you do try it, stitch the piping and border to the triangles before constructing the squares.

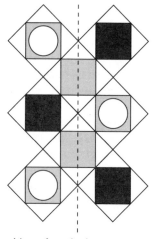

Line of vertical symmetry

STEP 4:

a: Prepare backing triangles. You should have nine 14½" squares of batting left over if you made the full-size quilt, and four left over if you made the wallhanging. Cut one of the squares in fourths diagonally and the remaining in half diagonally.

Cut the 14½" template in half diagonally, and mark seam lines on the backing triangles you cut in Lesson One. Cut one triangle in half diagonally again and mark the seam lines on the four corner triangles. Baste the batting to the triangles as instructed in Lesson Two, General Instructions, page 23.

b: Safety pin the basted backing triangles to the arranged blocks to complete the rectangle.

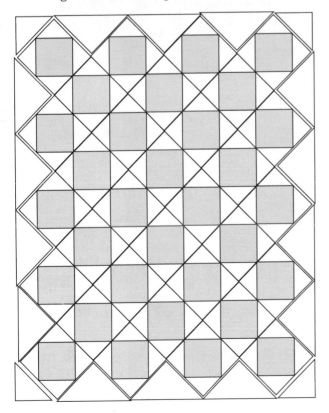

STEP 5:

Prepare blocks for stitching by using the 14½" square template from Lesson Two to check the marked seam lines. Re-mark them if necessary, since the quilting may have distorted the block. Stitch the blocks together in the following sequence.

Stitch four rows together, then repeat starting from the opposite corner. The last seam to be stitched will be in the center of the quilt.

a: Begin in one corner. Unpin the corner block and the attached triangles. Remove the basting stitches holding the batting as you stitch each seam, and hold the batting out of the way so you don't catch it. Pin the seam lines together, and then machine

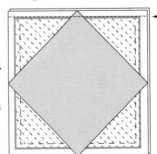

Stitching Line

stitch from one edge of the fabric to the other. Trim the seam to a generous ¼"; then finger press open.

b. Trim the edges of the batting if necessary, so that they just meet but do not overlap. Catch stitch the edges together.

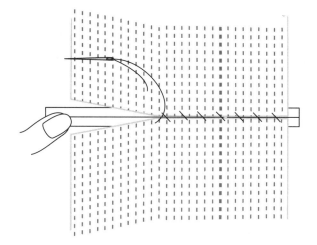

c. Unpin the next diagonal row of blocks and stitch it together in the same fashion. Stitch that row to the corner unit, again making sure not to stitch batting into the seam, and matching seams at the corners. Trim the seam and finger press open. Fold the border over the batting and safety pin to protect it while you are stitching the setting squares.

STEP 6:

Add the setting squares: (This is where you will make adjustments for differing block sizes.) Make a 10½" square template of cardboard or plastic. Finger press the seam allowance of the setting squares over the edges of the template.

Pin a setting square in place over the exposed batting square, lining up the finger-pressed seam allowances over the seam lines of the constructed blocks. If necessary, adjust the seam line of the setting square. (The seam allowance at the edge of the quilt should not be turned under or appliqued. Baste it in place.)

At the corners where the blocks meet, turn under a diagonal fold from the corner of one constructed block to the next. Applique the block in place, stitching through all layers.

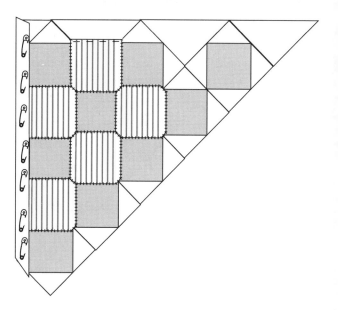

Add the setting squares as you add each row of blocks. This makes it easier to do the hand sewing. You may wish to add quilting to these squares. I would suggest a fairly simple design such as concentric squares, since the seam allowances in the back will be difficult to stitch through.

Stitch four diagonal rows together to make two halves, then stitch the last row and add the setting squares.

STEP 7:

Measure and mark the borders. Measure the side edges of the quilt top, not including the backing and batting, from seam line to seam line. Average the measurement (if one edge is 72" and one is 73", use 72½"). Add ½" for seam allowance, and cut the top and bottom borders to that length.

Repeat measurement for the top and bottom borders, but before cutting, add 11" plus 1" for seam allowance.

On the wrong side of the fabric, mark a ¼" seam allowance on the inner edge.

Make two stencils for the quilting pattern, one for the corner flower and one for the vine design, using Pattern A on page 232 and Pattern C on page 234. (Pattern B is simply Pattern A flipped over; the same stencil can be used.) Use either lightweight cardboard or template plastic. Cut a 5½" square for the corner, and a 5½" x 10¼" strip for the vine. Trace the pattern on the stencil material, and then cut a narrow channel with a craft knife or mat knife. Be sure to leave "bridges" so that the center parts of the design don't fall out.

Mark the quilting pattern on the right side of the fabric with the stencils. If desired, the pattern may be traced on the fabric instead.

For the side borders, mark a ½" seam allowance at each end and divide the remaining amount evenly by the number of rows of blocks. Mark the divisions on the wrong side and press creases in the borders at each mark. For the top and bottom

borders, mark ½" from each end, then 5" for the corner square.

The vine is flipped each time it is marked, so that it twines from one side of the border to the other. Keep in mind that you will probably want the flowers to be stem down on each side of the quilt, and the vine to be symmetrical. You may also

Side borders — Pattern B, Pattern A

Top and bottom borders — Pattern B, Pattern C, Pattern C, Pattern A

want the flowers to go in different directions on the top and bottom, but the vines should be symmetrical again.

You will probably have to adjust the pattern and placement of the individual flowers to fit your block measurements. If you mark lightly, or with a removable line, you can change your mind more easily. Mark the corner flowers on each end of the top and bottom borders, and then extend the vine markings to touch them.

Alternate:
I designed the quilting pattern from the pattern in the striped fabric I used for the setting squares. If you wish, try designing your own pattern. Make it the size of the divided border measurement from above. If you have used striped fabric for the setting squares, you may want to use it for the borders as well, simplifying the quilting pattern.

STEP 8:

Stitch the borders to the quilt. Lay the quilt out on a table with the side edge of the quilt flat. Line up the pressed creases for the end seam lines with the seam lines of the top and bottom blocks. Distribute the fabric evenly, and pin closely, about every ½", making sure the marked seam lines of the border and block line up. Stitch on the seam line. Open out the border fabric and baste close to the inside and outside edges and down the center. Safety pins may be used for the basting.

Repeat with the other side border.

Lay the quilt out again, with the top edge flat. Line up the pressed creases for the corner square with the seam lines of the side border and pin in place. Adjust the fabric and pin as above, then stitch, open and baste as you did for the side borders.

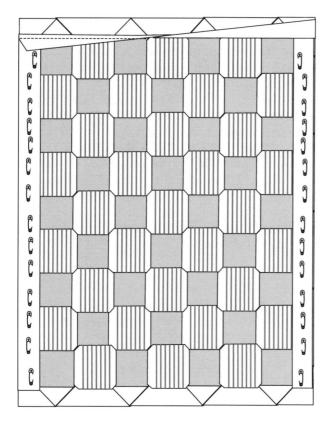

STEP 9:

Quilt the borders. You may find it helpful to use a small frame.

STEP 10:

After quilting is complete, use a yardstick to mark straight edges and square corners. If necessary, rebaste the edges, then trim all layers.

Add the binding.

a: Measure the outside edge of the quilt, and cut and stitch 2" straight grain strips to equal the measurement plus at least 12", joining strips on the diagonal. Press the strip in half lengthwise, wrong sides together.

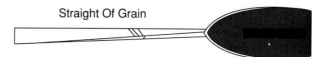

Straight Of Grain

b: Starting about 10" from a corner and leaving 4" of binding free, machine stitch the binding to the right side of the quilt top, matching raw edges and using a scant ¼" seam. Be sure that batting comes all the way to the raw edge. Add small pieces if necessary.

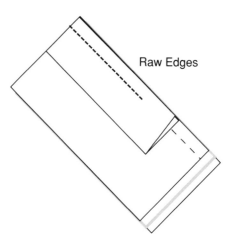

Raw Edges

c: When you come to a corner, stop stitching ¼"
from the edge and remove the work from the
machine. Fold and pleat the binding so that the
raw edges follow the raw edges of the quilt.
Begin stitching again at the top edge, pleating
the under layer diagonallly.

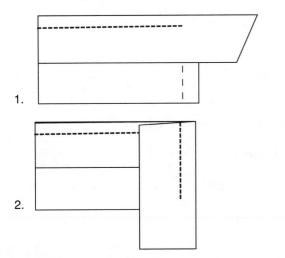

1.

2.

d: When you get within 2 " of where the stitching
began, stop and remove the work from the
machine. Place both ends of the binding along
the raw edges, and mark a spot where they
overlap with pins. Unfold and join the binding
in a diagonal seam, matching the pins as
shown. Trim the seam, then finish stitching the
binding to the top.

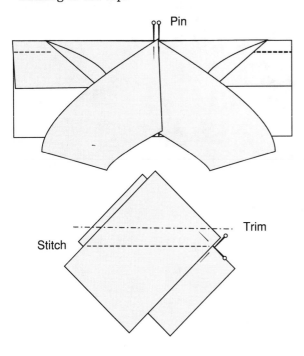

Pin

Stitch

Trim

e: Turn the binding over the raw edge and
applique over the stitching line. Be careful not
to let stitches show on the top. At the corners,
pull the binding out flat, forming a triangle,
then fold it back over the corner to miter it.

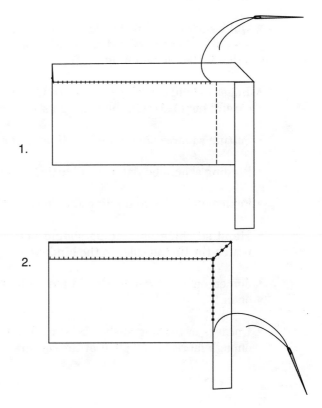

1.

2.

HOW ARE YOU DOING?

When you have finished your quilt, check it to see how you are doing.

• Quilt should lie flat. Blocks must be joined on the marked seam lines, and the seams should be finger pressed open. You may find it helpful to lay the pieces to be joined on a flat surface for pinning.

• Edges should not ripple. Be sure to measure carefully before cutting the borders. Be careful not to stretch them as you stitch the binding on.

• Setting squares should lie flat. If necessary, add some quilting to them.

• Binding should be flat, full of batting and even in width.

• Folded and stitched binding should cover the machine stitching used to apply it.

• Hand stitching on binding should not show. Use small, close applique stitches, and match the thread color to the binding.

• Joined ends of binding should not be bulky. Use a diagonal seam, and trim and press open.

• Corners of binding should be smoothly mitered and stitched closed. Be sure to leave enough fabric in the pleat at the corners.

SECTION TWO:

Constructing a Top and Then

Basting It on a Frame

Fabric Required

It does not take as much fabric for the background, border and backing for this method. You will need:

> 10 yards for the full-size quilt
>
> 3¾ yards for the wallhanging

Use the cutting diagrams to cut the fabric pieces needed.

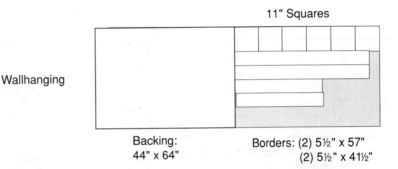

Full-size

11" Squares

Backing: (2) 44" x 104"   Borders: (2) 5 ½" x 92 ½"
(2) 5 ½" x 82 ½"

11" Squares

Wallhanging

Backing: 44" x 64"   Borders: (2) 5½" x 57"
(2) 5½" x 41½"

Modify the instructions given for each lesson as follows:

Lesson Two: Mark the quilting patterns on the blocks as directed. You can still use masking tape to quilt the Starflower, Pattern A, after the quilt is in the frame. Join these blocks to the other blocks as directed on page 228.

Lesson Three: Construct blocks.

Lesson Four: Construct blocks.

Lesson Five: Mark the quilting patterns on the blocks as directed. Join them to the other blocks as directed on page 228. You will probably want to hand stitch the designs using the techniques from Lesson Two.

Lesson Six: Construct blocks.

Lesson Seven: Construct blocks.

Lesson Eight: Prepare the blocks for quilting as instructed. Cording in Pattern D, Ring of Roses, should be done after the entire quilt is quilted.

Lesson Nine: Construct blocks.

STEP 1:

Trim all blocks to 10½" squares, with seam allowances of ¼". Use the 10" square template to mark seam lines on the back of each block. If constructed blocks measure less than 10½", add a narrow border to bring them to size.

Cut the setting squares 10½" square. (31 for the full-size quilt, 7 for the wallhanging.) Use the 10" square template to mark seam lines on the wrong side of the fabric.

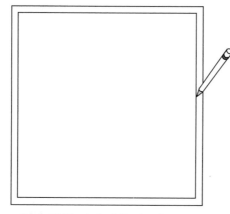

Back Of Block And Setting Square

STEP 2:

Arrange the blocks and setting squares following the instructions in Section One. When you are satisfied with the layout, pin the seam allowances together temporarily.

STEP 3:

Stitch the blocks and setting squares for each row together by machine, pinning the seam lines at the corners and along the marked line. Stitch from one edge to the other. Press seams toward the setting squares.

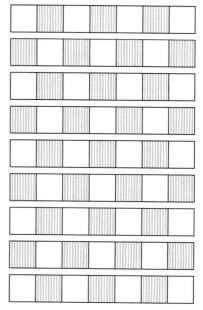

Stitch the rows together, making sure that the seams match in the corners. Press the seams in one direction.

STEP 4:

Measure the side and top and bottom edges for borders as in Section One, and mark the quilting design as described. When the marking is complete, pin the border pieces to the sides of the top, matching the ends of the seam and pinning the marked seam lines together. Stitch and press toward the border.

Pin the border pieces to the top and bottom, matching the seam lines of the side borders with the pressed crease for the corner. Pin the marked seam lines together. Stitch and press toward the border.

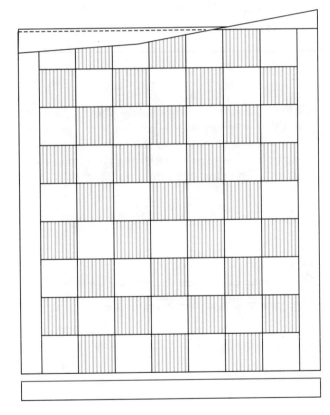

STEP 5:

Construct the backing. It should be exactly 4" wider and longer than the quilt top, measured across the center in each direction.

You will need to use two lengths of fabric for the full-size quilt backing. Split one length of the backing fabric and stitch the two pieces to opposite sides of the remaining length. Be sure not to reverse the grain.

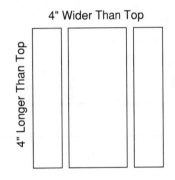

STEP 6:

Baste the quilt layers.

a: Make a simple basting frame from 10' lengths of 1" x 2" boards and four C-clamps. It can be supported on the backs of four kitchen chairs. If the wood is soft enough to thumbtack into, use that method to attach the backing. If not, staple or tack folded strips of muslin or another sturdy fabric to one edge of each board to provide a place to pin. Make a rectangle of the boards and C-clamps approximately the measurement of the quilt backing.

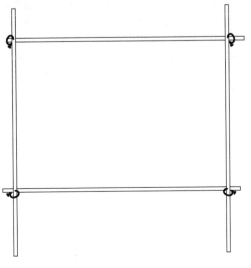

b: Begin in one corner to attach the backing to the frame. Use a book or other right angle to make sure the corner is square, then pin or thumbtack the backing even with the inner or outer edge of the board. Work in both directions from the corner. Do not pull too hard on the cross grain of the fabric as you stretch it, since it is easy to distort.

When you reach the next corners, square them using the same tool and work toward the last corner. When all the sides of the backing are attached to the frame, measure them to make sure they are even.

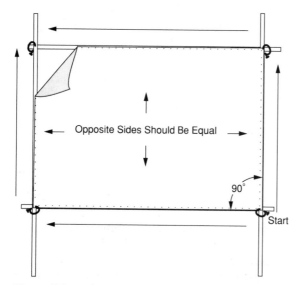

c: If possible, take the batting out of the package a day early and spread it out to rest. After the backing is attached to the frame, unroll the batting over the backing, trimming it if necessary to fit inside the frame. Pat out any bumps or creases, and gently adjust it. Be careful not to distort it by pulling on it.

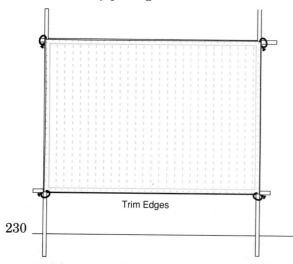

d: Fold the finished top in fourths, wrong side out, and lay it on a corner of the batting and backing. Carefully unfold it, avoiding dragging it over the batting if possible. Adjust it so that it lies flat, and the edges are an even distance from the edge of the frame.

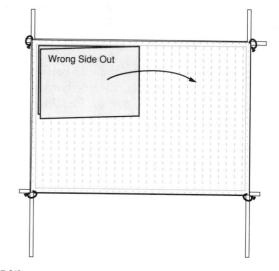

e: I like to use small brass safety pins for basting, but you may use thread basting if you prefer. Pin or baste the edges of the quilt first, making sure the edges are straight and the corners are square. Then pin or baste as far in as you can reach.

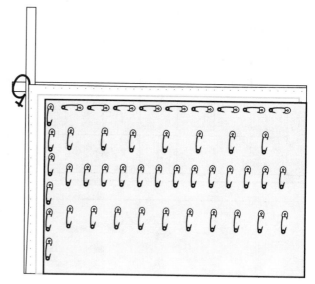

f: When you can't reach any farther, remove the C-clamps at the end of the top boards, and carefully roll them up as far as has been basted. Then replace the clamps and continue. Work in this manner until the entire surface is pinned or basted.

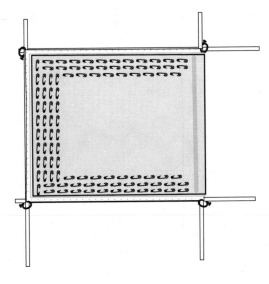

STEP 7:

Remove the quilt from the basting frame and quilt. You may use a floor frame, a hoop, or do it in your lap or on a table. Follow the instructions for quilting the blocks in Lesson Two and Lesson Eight, and use hand quilting for the patterns in Lesson Five.

STEP 8:

When the quilting is complete, bind the edges as described in Section One.

Tips for Quilting on a Frame:
- It will take practice to be able to stitch smoothly in all directions, but it is worth the effort.
- Be careful about leaving sharp scissors on the quilt top. It's easy to have an accident.
- You will probably have to experiment to find a combination of chair height and frame height that is comfortable for you.

PATTERN A

PATTERN B

PATTERN C

LECTURE: CARE OF FINISHED QUILTS

If you give your finished quilt reasonable care, it will last a long time. Not forever, but depending on how much it is used, it may well outlive you. The basic rules are: keep it clean and store it properly.

Keep It Clean

If you washed all your fabrics before using them and are sure they will not run or shrink, there is no reason you can't gently wash your finished quilt. There are mild detergents available at quilt shops which can be used, and a gentle cycle in your washer will not hurt it. Do not use high heat to dry a quilt, however; it might shrink or melt a polyester batt. I prefer to air-dry a quilt if possible, supporting it over two or three clotheslines, and turning it frequently.

If your quilt is not washable, or you are concerned about one or more of the fabrics in it, it can be dry-cleaned. Be sure to spread it out to air for a day or so after you get it back, to make sure all lingering chemicals are gone.

The frequency of washing or dry-cleaning depends on use. A quilt doesn't need washing just because it's dusty; shake it out and air it to clean it. On the other hand, if the fabric is getting soiled, clean it right away so the dirt doesn't become set.

Store It Properly

The best long-term storage for a quilt is flat, but few of us have extra beds to keep them on, or long tubes to roll them on the way museums do. Folds can weaken the fabric and crease the batting, as well as fade if they are exposed to light. If you need to fold a quilt to store it for a long period, there are a couple of things you can do to minimize the problems. First of all, take the quilt out of storage every six months or so, shake out the folds, and let it rest unfolded for a day or two. When you fold it again, fold it in different places. That is, if you folded it down the middle the long way before, fold it in thirds this time. You can also stuff the folds with acid-free tissue paper to prevent creases from developing. Don't use regular tissue paper for extended storage; the acid in it will weaken the fabric. For the same reason, don't store quilts in cardboard boxes or wooden chests or drawers. The best container is an acid-free storage box.

Quilts definitely should not be stored in plastic bags or boxes. The plastic will not let the fibers breathe, and mold, mildew, and mustiness are likely to occur. In addition, plastic garbage bags with quilts in them are easily mistaken for trash, and every quilter knows a horror story.

If you take good care of your finished quilt, it should last a long time, and give you great satisfaction whenever you use it.

RESOURCES

First Aid for Family Quilts, Nancy O'Bryant Puentes, Moon Over The Mountain Publishing.
Protecting Your Quilts: An Owner's Guide to Insurance, Care and Restoration, and Appraisal, American Quilter's Society Appraisal Certification Committee, AQS, Paducah, KY, 1990.

American Quilter's Society

dedicated to publishing books for today's quilters

The following AQS publications are currently available:

American Beauties: Rose & Tulip Quilts
by Gwen Marston & Joe Cunningham
#1907: AQS, 1988, 96 pages, softbound, $14.95

America's Pictorial Quilts by Caron L. Mosey
#1662: AQS, 1985, 112 pages, hardbound, $19.95

Applique Designs: My Mother Taught Me to Sew
by Faye Anderson
#2121: AQS, 1990, 80 pages, softbound, $12.95

Arkansas Quilts: Arkansas Warmth
Arkansas Quilter's Guild, Inc.
#1908: AQS, 1987, 144 pages, hardbound, $24.95

The Art of Hand Appliqué by Laura Lee Fritz
#2122: AQS, 1990, 80 pages, softbound, $14.95

..Ask Helen More About Quilting Designs by Helen Squire
#2099: AQS, 1990, 54 pages, 17x11, spiral-bound, $14.95

Collection of Favorite Quilts, A by Judy Florence
#2119 AQS, 1990, 136 pages, softbound, $18.95

Dear Helen, Can You Tell Me? ...all about quilting designs
by Helen Squire
#1820: AQS, 1987, 56 pages, 17 x 11, spiral-bound, $12.95

Dyeing & Overdyeing of Cotton Fabrics by Judy Mercer Tescher
#2030: AQS, 1990, 54 pages, softbound, $9.95

Fun & Fancy Machine Quiltmaking by Lois Smith
#1982: AQS, 1989, 144 pages, softbound, $19.95

Gallery of American Quilts: 1849-1988
#1938: AQS, 1988, 128 pages, softbound, $19.95

Gallery of American Quilts 1860-1989: Book II
#2129: AQS, 1990, 128 pages, softbound, $19.95

The Grand Finale: A Quilter's Guide to Finishing Projects
by Linda Denner
#1924: AQS, 1988, 96 pages, softbound, $14.95

Heirloom Miniatures by Tina M. Gravatt
#2097: AQS, 1990, 64 pages, softbound, $9.95

Home Study Course in Quiltmaking by Jeannie M. Spears
#2031: AQS, 1990, 240 pages, softbound, $19.95

The Ins and Outs: Perfecting the Quilting Stitch
by Patricia J. Morris
#2120: AQS, 1990, 96 pages, softbound, $9.95

Irish Chain Quilts: A Workbook of Irish Chains & Related Patterns by Joyce B. Peaden
#1906: AQS, 1988, 96 pages, softbound, $14.95

Missouri Heritage Quilts by Bettina Havig
#1718: AQS, 1986, 104 pages, softbound, $14.95

Nancy Crow: Quilts and Influences by Nancy Crow
#1981: AQS, 1990, 256 pages, hardcover, $29.95

No Dragons on My Quilt by Jean Ray Laury with
Ritva Laury and Lizabeth Laury
#2153: AQS, 1990, 52 pages, hardcover, $12.95

Oklahoma Heritage Quilts
Oklahoma Quilt Heritage Project
#2032: AQS, 1990, 144 pages, softbound, $19.95

Scarlet Ribbons: American Indian Technique for Today's Quilters by Helen Kelley
#1819: AQS, 1987, 104 pages, softbound, $15.95

Sets & Borders by Gwen Marston and Joe Cunningham
#1821: AQS, 1987, 104 pages, softbound, $14.95

Somewhere in Between: Quilts and Quilters of Illinois
by Rita Barrow Barber
#1790: AQS, 1986, 78 pages, softbound, $14.95

Stenciled Quilts for Christmas by Marie Monteith Sturmer
#2098: AQS, 1990, 104 pages, softbound, $14.95

Texas Quilts–Texas Treasures
Texas Heritage Quilt Society
#1760: AQS, 1986, 160 pages, hardbound, $24.95

Treasury of Quilting Designs, A by Linda Goodmon Emery
#2029: AQS, 1990, 80 pages, 14"x11", spiral-bound, $14.95

These books can be found in local bookstores and quilt shops. If you are unable to locate a title in your area, you can order by mail from AQS, P.O. Box 3290, Paducah, KY 42002-3290. Please add $1 for the first book and 40¢ for each additional one to cover postage and handling.

746.9
~~646.9~~ SPE   8/93

Spears, Jeannie M.
Home study course in
quiltmaking.